John Mayall

Blues Breaker

Cover Photograph: Redferns

Photographs: Pictorial Press, Redferns

Printed by: Staples of Rochester, Kent.

Copyright: Richard Newman 1995

Published by Castle Communications plc, A29 Barwell Business Park,
Leatherhead Road, Chessington, Surrey KT9 2NY.

While the publishers have made every reasonable effort to trace the
copyright owners for any or all of the photographs in this book, there
may be some omissions of credits for which we apologise.

ISBN: 1 86074 129 0

John Mayall
Blues Breaker

by
Richard Newman

This book is dedicated to John Joyce
(guitar repairer and twelve-string guitar virtuoso) and
Gerry Southard (owner of Potters Music Shop, Richmond),
for help, guidance and education over the years.

Acknowledgements

Richard Newman would like to thank first and foremost Alice Neaves for her patience and perseverance under fire; also his long suffering family who have just about had enough of the sixties by now. In addition, thanks to Mark Wingfield and Penny Braybrooke for their encouragement with this project.

Foreword

One of the big problems for a guitar teacher like myself comes when you try to give your students a sense of culture with regard to the blues and the guitar in general. This is especially true of the British blues scene. Where did it all come from? Who did Eric Clapton listen to? Why was there a British blues scene at all? And what happened to it? Every student guitarist that I come across has heard of Eric Clapton and many have heard of some of the great black American blues performers. However, hardly any of them, quite understandably, have much idea of the bigger picture.

Richard Newman's book puts it all together for us and traces the roots and connections of the London blues scene, which ultimately led to some of the finest blues performances of all time. The book also shows the part that John Mayall played in this movement and the reason that he is known to so many throughout the world. This is not a book dedicated to those obsessed with the cold dry facts of history; more it is for anyone who is trying to gain a view of the bigger picture. Read and enjoy.

Mark Wingfield
Guitar teacher and jazz musician
Cambridge, August 1995

Contents

Preface

One evening in February 1973, there was a ring on my doorbell. I was living in a bedsit in Kew Gardens (a leafy suburb of West London), world famous for its botanical gardens. The house in which my bedsit was located contained a number of other flats and a payphone down in the hall. I wandered down to the front door and on opening it was greeted by the sight of a short man, well built, wearing a woolly fishing hat and carrying a guitar in what appeared to be two old potato sacks. He said: 'Are you Richard Newman? My name is Geoff Bradford.'

This was a life-changing moment. I had read about these life-changing moments in many books, but never expected to experience one myself. You see, the point was I was just a fan – one of many who would turn up at folk clubs, rock concerts and university gigs and watch the musicians on stage perform their own particular magic. Kew Gardens is just down the road from Richmond in Surrey, which is where my parents had their house. At the bottom of Richmond Hill, just before you came to the cinema, was a record shop called Potters Music Shop. Since the middle of 1967, I had done my very best to be its best customer and had probably succeeded.

In 1967, I was seventeen years old and the one thing on my mind was to learn to play the guitar so that I could meet girls. If you had been living in Richmond at that time you would have immediately understood my problem. The hippie revolution, or an extremely watered down middle-class version of the hippie revolution, was in full swing. I have never seen girls so beautiful since that time and the only place you can go today to see an equivalent is the university town of

Cambridge, just after the beginning of term. Now to a young man of seventeen years fresh out of Battersea (a working class area of South London best known for its power station), the quest to meet young girls was the dominating influence that invaded daily thoughts.

Little did I know at the time that I was walking around a trail that another had trodden some years before. This trail included Potters Music Shop, Richmond Green, the River Thames at Richmond and a cafe (la Burge), which was sandwiched between Potters Music on one side and the cinema on the other.

Right from the start I was a complete romantic and lived life mostly in my imagination, which had little to do with the practicalities of daily life. I had had a series of very good jobs working in computers, which culminated in a job at ICL in Putney – just down the road from Richmond. I was not starving and to my knowledge had never had the blues – apart, that is, from my longing for female company. Oh yes, that original trail blazer to whom I was referring turned out to be a fellow romantic, but the difference between us was that he had had plenty in his life to have the blues about. His name was Eric Clapton!

Back to Geoff Bradford... By the time Geoff had rung my door bell in 1973, I had purchased through Potters Music Shop a comprehensive collection of blues albums and virtually every book obtainable on learning to play the guitar, the history of blues guitar and the blues in general. I was your archetypal bookworm and very, very serious about the blues. Geoff and I climbed the stairs into my palatial mansion.

The reason that he had come was to audition for a spot on a radio programme that I was compiling for Capital Radio, London's first commercial music radio station. At the time the programme, *Night Flight*, was being presented and produced by Robbie Barish (now a Doctor of Physics and an authority on the effects of radiation from the sun on airline passengers), who was a veteran presenter on WBAI in New York. WBAI is part of the Pacifica Radio network, which is kept on the air in America by public subscription. It was on this station that Bob Dylan, Joan Baez and many others got their first radio broadcast.

Geoff removed his guitar from the two potato sacks and explained to me that he hadn't got a case and, in fact, that he had borrowed the guitar. He said this to me as if it was a completely normal situation. Since the room was so small he was forced to sit on the bed, and I remember making him a cup of tea. It was clear from the start that

Geoff was very working class and so, of course, was I. (My father had been a window cleaner and was now a London taxi driver.) This turned out to be very fortuitous since unknown to me, Geoff Bradford was famous among his peers for his left-wing political views – many of which I genuinely shared with him. Having finished his tea he then proceeded to play his borrowed guitar.

Now you must understand the situation clearly: here is an older man playing to a younger man; they have only just met. The younger man – me – had spent the years between 1967 and 1973 deep in a passionate and romantic study of the blues. The older man, though I didn't realise it at the time, had virtually given up playing the guitar. As soon as Geoff Bradford began to play, though, I realised that my life would never be the same again.

Although I knew my stuff as far as the blues is concerned, and although I had been to many, many concerts by that time, I had never seen anything like his playing. He was, to understate matters, a complete acoustic guitar genius. He started to play Blind Blake ragtime pieces – notably 'Southern Rag'. In a sense it was lucky for Geoff that I knew so much about this obscure music and was able to recognise immediately the quality of his playing. The average radio person's knowledge of this art form would perhaps understandably if written down not fit on to the proverbial postage stamp.

To understate matters yet again, I was completely amazed!

We began to talk and we got on straight away. To the outside world we presented the perfect contrast: Geoff, a quietly confident mature man; and me, a rather loud romantic enthusiast who had somehow managed against all the odds to be in charge of putting together a series of live seven-hour radio programmes.

You see, the most curious fact is that if there was any musical justice in the world, Geoff Bradford would have been known to millions by then. As it was hardly anybody knew anything about him. During that conversation I found out that he had been the original Rolling Stones lead guitarist. He had been invited to join a new group by a young slide guitar player from Cheltenham who looked more like a choirboy than a blues man. The 'choirboy's' name was Brian Jones. However, as far as Geoff Bradford was concerned Brian Jones was eventually to make a bad mistake by inviting to a rehearsal a young, scrawny black-haired boy who *did* look like a blues player, but strangely enough wanted to play Chuck Berry. A line had to be drawn somewhere and for Geoff Bradford, already a virtuoso electric guitar player, playing Chuck Berry represented that line. The Chuck Berry enthusiast was Keith Richards. Geoff immediately left the rehearsals – and the rest you probably know about.

Some time afterwards Geoff Bradford had a nervous breakdown. It was a case of too many one night stands with the Blues By Six, the band in which he was playing (more of which later). His doctor had ordered him off the road. Drugs had played a part in this situation and although Geoff was not involved in hard drugs, he had been taking stimulants of various different kinds to keep him going.

Ironically, as was often the case, this was to stop his career at the very moment that it could have taken off in a big way. While lying flat on his back, literally, he received a phone call from another band leader asking him if he would like to join his group. That phone call came from John Mayall.

This book tells a very strange story. It's the story of how a tiny, very English, very London, very West London, blues scene was to have a major influence on the whole blues rock explosion that took place throughout the western world in the ten years between 1964 and 1974. It is also about the vision of three very different people who had a coincidental coming together that is strange in itself.

Most people reading this book who are of a certain age – that is, getting on a little bit – will recognise instantly our three visionaries: John Mayall, Eric Clapton and Peter Green. However, I wonder how many of you would equally recognise the names Cyril Davies or Geoff Bradford. Very few I am sure.

That phone call from John Mayall to Geoff Bradford is very significant because it represented a potential link between one generation of blues players with a new generation of blues enthusiasts who, in West London, were beginning at that time to discover the blues. However, it was Eric Clapton who got the job, and that single fact was to transform this new audience's perception of how the blues should be played.

What no one was expecting was that this perception would be changed again in a very short space of time by a working class East London street kid with a manic belief in his ability, who was determined 'to get alongside' Eric Clapton. This, of course, was Peter Green.

In this book I will seek to make connections from the history of blues to show a direction in the art form, both in the performance of the music of the blues and in the coincidence of events in blues history that led inevitably to the moment when John Mayall was to form his Bluesbreakers. What I aim to show is that John Mayall, with his deep knowledge and heartfelt passion for blues music and his professionalism as a band leader, was a major part of the London blues scene, which in turn was an important element of a world-wide movement that still continues to spread the gospel of the blues even today.

It is not possible to appreciate John Mayall's contribution without an overview of the development of blues in America and of the early blues scene in West London. It's an exciting journey and perhaps will give you some food for thought.

In his sleeve notes for the 1967 album *Crusade*, John Mayall said the following.

'I have chosen to campaign for some of my blues heroes by recording one number each from their own recorded repertoires and amongst the original compositions I include a tribute to J.B. Lenoir whose untimely death came as a great shock to me. I was even more saddened by the fact that his death only rated a couple of brief paragraphs in one British musical paper and it seems that his short life was one of great work without reward.

'It is about time that the blues fraternity made an outcry against the system locked in the belief that blues fans are only a small minority in the world of popular music. Hence the title of this new Bluesbreakers LP Crusade*. I have dedicated my life to the blues... I hope you will join forces with me.'*

Clearly John Mayall believed from the start that it was important for any new blues fan to gain an understanding and an education with regard to the roots of the music and the development of blues culture.

In a recent interview with *Guitar Player* magazine, John Mayall said while talking about Jimi Hendrix: 'The drag is that those people who worship Hendrix rarely go back a step or two to find out where Jimi was getting his stuff. If they did they'd have a better idea of what it was all about. If you listen to Muddy Waters you would have a clue as to where 'Voodoo Chile' came from.'

This book is not a biography. Rather, it is an attempt to draw a map that will lead the reader to check out the roots of Mayall and to understand better the London blues scene. It also attempts to provide an insight into the pivotal role that John Mayall played in giving an oportunity to a new generation of players at a time when what they needed most was such a champion.

John Mayall marched through the sixties behind his banner. He was a crusader for the blues. He was determined to break the blues. He was a BLUESBREAKER!

This journey through the landscape of the blues is one that along with John Mayall and many others, I have taken myself, at least intellectually and as a musician. It has enriched my life and taught me much of what I know of this world.

There is a great deal of truth in the blues...

Richard Newman
Cambridgeshire, England
August 1995

Part I

Chapter 1

Dark was the night...
American blues

At the end of the nineteen century in the southern states of the United States of America The Blues came into existence. And this is where they all started. This is the root for all of them... for John Mayall, Eric Clapton and Peter Green. The blues was from the start a form of entertainment and it is important to remember this. The early blues men were not even aware of the concept of the 'blues man' preferring to see themselves as 'songsters'.

At that time, the life of the average black American was not that far removed from the worst excesses of slavery. There has been much speculation as to the origins of the blues musical form. Some say it originated in Africa, others say it's a fusion of western musical styles (such as Scottish and Irish ballads), ragtime dance pieces, early country and western music... and so on. Wherever it came from no one will have known anything about it outside of the rural ghettos in which it was originally performed had it not been for a technological innovation – the invention of the phonograph.

Perhaps the first musician really to have any kind of influence through this new media was Charley Patton. Patton was born in April 1891 in Edwards, Mississippi. The world in which he was to play his music was one of poverty, squalor, illiteracy and violence. Life was cheap and at the time disputes between black males on a Saturday night at the many 'juke joints' that were the venues for the performance of blues music, were settled with the gun or the knife. Blues music was considered the Devil's Music. No self-respecting upstanding member of any black community at that time, could be seen to have anything to do with this music.

What we need to remember from the start is that the blues man and the music itself represented a counter culture to the establishment represented by the church. A juke joint was a shack or some kind of outhouse building, almost invariably off the beaten track and as far out of the sight of the local respectable white and black population as could be arranged. What you did at a juke joint was dance, drink and hopefully by the end of the evening end up with a sexual partner. One of the dances of the time, 'The Slow Drag', scandalised the respectable churchgoing community. It involved much grinding of bodies together in an overtly sexual way and very quickly determined whether your chosen partner was interested in taking matters further. As the evening proceeded and inevitably the dancers consumed more and more alcohol, fights would break out which very often resulted in someone dead on the dance floor.

The guitarist singer would sit in the corner and play his instrument. He would be plied with alcohol and encouraged by a group of women who would inevitably surround him, egging him on. Many of these girls would have male partners who were drinking not more than a few feet away. If the singer wasn't very careful he could easily end up dead on the dance floor himself as a result of the aggression of a jealous reveller.

Blues lyrics tended to document the trials and troubles of sexual relationships. It was rare for the lyrical content of a blues to take as its subject matter a current event or happening. However, Charley Patton was one of the first recorded blues men to take this course. Patton would inject a personal viewpoint into his music in such titles as 'Pony Blues' (a song about travelling), 'High Sheriff Blues' (which dealt with imprisonment) and 'Highwater Everywhere' (dealing with floods).

Patton also lived the life of the classic blues man. He drank and smoked, and legend has it that he had a total of eight wives. He would boast of his sexual conquests and demanded to be the centre of attention. He was aggressive and belligerent and travelled extensively. He was the proverbial rolling stone who never stayed in one place for too long. He was also superstitious, and was jailed at least once. However, he was an immense influence on a line of musicians who were to follow him down a road that in many ways he was the first to tread. Another curious fact about Charley Patton is that he was a very animated performer. He would play the guitar between his knees and behind his back and would often use the guitar like a drum, slapping and banging it during performance.

Patton had grown up in the Mississippi hill country and had been taken at an early age down to the Delta to work on the Dockery plantation. It was here that he came in to contact with Henry Sloane, one of the first Delta blues men. Sloane never got an opportunity to record, but was by all accounts an influence on Patton.

As time passed Patton began to develop his own style and by 1915 or thereabouts he was becoming the Delta's most popular blues man, his reputation based on his personality as much as his music. He was to play at picnics, parties and at levee camps as well as at the infamous juke joints. By this time he had formed a friendship with fellow guitarist Willie Brown.

Charley Patton finally got his chance to record in 1929 after he had auditioned for Henry Speir, a music store owner from Jackson, Mississippi. Speir was in fact a talent scout whose job was to look out for local recordable black performers.

By the 1920s many black homes in rural communities either had, or had access to, wind-up gramophones. These were machines that gave an adequate if not slightly primitive sound reproduction. However, to the rural fieldworker they were a revelation, allowing him or her for the first time to hear music from outside their local community. Paramount Records was one of the first companies to exploit this new market. The records it released to this market were known as 'race records' because the black community was known as The Race. At first sight this may appear to be derogatory, but actually it merely signified a market – that is, the black community.

Patton first recorded in Richmond, Indiana and his first issued recording was 'Pony Blues'. The record sold very well, especially in the Delta region where he was already well known and 'Pony Blues' ultimately became known as his signature tune. In all Patton recorded fourteen sides in Indiana and was subsequently recalled by Paramount for a second session which took place in Grafton, Wisconsin at Paramount's home studio. A Delta fiddle player called Henry Son Simms accompanied him on fiddle.

During the 1930s Paramount issued thirteen Patton records and thus Charlie Patton became a country blues star. He was to record again and on one session he cut 'O Death', which was to prove prophetic. A few months after committing this song to record he died of a heart condition. He was forty-three years old.

On many occasions when Patton was performing in the Delta he was joined by Willie Brown and by another younger performer, Son House. Eddie James Junior (*aka* Son House) was born on 21 March, 1902 making him eleven years Charley Patton's junior. Son House had an interest in religion and was a preacher as well as a blues singer and performer. He actually became a Baptist pastor by the time he turned twenty. Trying to maintain a balance between the sacred and secular worlds was obviously going to lead to trouble, which it did with women and alcohol. Son House had one of the most aggressive blues guitar styles of that time and he sang with enormous emotion. Although influenced by Charley Patton and also by the emotion contained in church worship of the time he rapidly developed his own style. He was to team up with Willie Brown and they played many engagements together.

Son House spent some time in Louisiana in the early 1920s. He returned to the Delta in 1926 and learned how to play the guitar. He worked local juke joints as well as the levee camps and house parties, but in 1928 he shot and killed a man.

House was sent to Parchment Farm, a Mississippi penitentiary with an infamous reputation. However, a year later he got lucky when a judge re-examined his case and ordered that he should be released from prison. Eventually, House arrived at Lula, Mississippi where he was to meet Charley Patton and Willie Brown.

House in effect became part of Charley Patton's circle and he actually ended up recording some tracks himself for the Paramount label, one of which was called 'Preaching The Blues'. This was an account of how the blues stole his soul away from the church, a familiar theme at the time being that the blues was the Devil's music.

Superstition was an everyday part of life in the Delta, and making a pact with the Devil was a way in which many blues performers were supposed to have gained their magical ability. The idea was that you would go to a crossroads at midnight with your guitar and sit and wait. Eventually a large black man would approach you and tune your guitar. What then followed was fame and fortune, women and booze, but at a price – that price often being betrayal, jealousy, bad luck and a violent, tragic death.

In 1941, Alan Lomax recorded Son House for the Library of Congress. He returned in 1942 to record House for a second time. However, the performer that Lomax was really looking for was a younger man by the name of Robert Johnson. A year after Lomax had recorded Son House, House moved to Rochester, New York and subsequently disappeared from the blues scene until 1964, when he was rediscovered.

Both Charley Patton and Son House had sung the blues with great emotional intensity. They had also been professional entertainers for the local community in which they lived. They had both been stars in the modern sense of the way we understand the phenomena. They both had charisma and were able to hold an audience, and people would flock to see them perform. Added to this they were an inspiration to a younger generation of musicians who were about to take the blues to a much wider audience and from the rural communities of the South into the cities of the North, most notably, Chicago. The musical inheritors of Patton's and House's 'culture of the blues' were two very different performers: Robert Johnson and Muddy Waters.

Chapter 2

Standing at the crossroads

Robert Johnson cut only twenty-nine tracks during his very brief recording career. Over the years since his death in 1938, his legend has grown and grown, and his influence on generations of musicians who have touched on the blues is incalculable.

Robert Johnson's father was one Noah Johnson. Robert was born on 8 May, 1911 in Hazelhurst, Mississippi to Julia Dodds as a result of an affair that she was having with Noah Johnson in Mr Dodd's absence. While Robert was still a baby his mother took him and his sister Karen and signed with a Delta labour supplier. For the next couple of years they lived an uncertain existence working in migrant labour camps. They were all living in Memphis with the family of one Charles Spencer. However, the Spencer house was full and in 1914, Charlie had a wife and a mistress, with children to both of them in addition to Robert.

Julia decided to leave her children and make her own way elsewhere. Memphis was Robert's home for the next couple of years and he lived with the Spencers in their Handwerker Hill residence. Robert was a strong-willed child, which led Mr Spencer eventually to decide that the child would do better under his mother's care. Robert was relocated to Robinsville, a small northern Mississippi cotton community forty miles south of Memphis. There he lived with his new stepfather, Willie 'Dusty' Willis, whom Julia had married in October 1916. Robert was raised by this couple to manhood.

Having taken the Spencer name, Robert Spencer (*aka* Johnson) began to take an interest in music. He started out with an interest in the Jew's harp and rapidly moved on to harmonica, which became his first musical obsession for the next few years. Robert had made friends with fellow musician R.L. Windum. They traded verses of songs and accompanied one another. This corporation seems to have continued until they were both young men.

When Robert was a teenager he was told about his real father and began introducing himself as Robert Johnson. He received a rudimentary education at the Indian Creek School at Commerce, Mississippi where the Willis's were then working on the Abbay and Leatherman plantation. Robert had trouble with his eyesight and this gave him an excuse to quit school. The problem with his eyes was to return from time to time over the years. His half-sister, Carrie, had bought some glasses for him in the early twenties in Helena, Arkansas but he never did get round to wearing them much. It appears that Robert had a small cataract, which affected him in one eye. However it later disappeared.

During the late 1920s Robert became interested in the guitar. He had made a rack for his harmonica out of baling wire and string and was able to pick out an accompaniment for his harmonica and voice to Leroy Carr's 1928 'How Long Blues', which was apparently one of his favourite songs at the time.

One of the most important points we need to note about Robert Johnson's early musical development is that he was one of the first new generation blues players to have access to records. By this time there was a considerable number of recordings of artists such as the previously mentioned Charley Patton, along with Blind Lemon Jefferson, coming on to the market. Jefferson was one of the most popular blues recording artists of that time. Robert Johnson went looking for other musicians from whom to learn. One of the local musicians who was regarded very highly was Willie Brown. Brown lived in Robinsville in those days and he tried to help Robert with the guitar by showing him all he could. Charley Patton regularly played in and around Robinsville, often, as has previously been noted, in the company of Willie Brown – and it was Patton who was to become a heavy influence on Robert Johnson.

Robert began playing music on a regular basis at this time. He was recycling the popular recorded blues of the day. However, he did not consider himself to be anything other than a farmer at this time. Also around this time he married Virginia Travis in Penton, Mississippi in February 1929. They started life together by sharing a home with Robert's older half-sister, Bessie and her husband, Granville Hinds. They lived on the Kline plantation, which was just east of Robinsville. In due course Virginia became pregnant and in the summer of 1929, Robert Johnson was a very proud expectant father. He obviously cared about Virginia a great deal. During a ride through the country in Granville Hinds' old car, Robert with some humour, recalled warning Granville when he hit a bad spot in the road to 'be careful man be careful! My wife's percolating.' However, tragedy was to strike for Johnson; Virginia and the baby died in childbirth in April 1930. She was sixteen years old and he was nineteen.

I suppose it's possible to try to imagine the effect on Robert's life of such a trauma; however, we would only be guessing. What we *do* know is that fate was about to deal another card.

Less than two months later, around about June, Son House came to live in Robinsville at the request of Willie Brown. With his combination of blues man and preacher, Son House's music had an intensity that was not even matched by Charley. Robert Johnson had never heard anything like it and we can imagine that in his traumatised state he was in the exact frame of mind to be heavily influenced by such emotional intensity. Robert began to follow Son House and Willie Brown wherever they went. He would find out where they were going to play and slip off on his own. Robert had been able to play some of Willie Brown's music, notably 'The Jinks Blues'. However, it was to Son House's music that Robert was now to turn.

In the end Robert became a bit of a nuisance to House and Brown; he would pick up one of their guitars whenever he could during a break in their performances, and play. The problem was he wasn't very good and Son House would warn him off.

Robert took the decision to work hard at his music because he had realised that if he wanted to become anything other than sharecropper (another name for a rural farmer at this time, which stemmed from the practice of sharing the income from the crop with a white landowner who would bank-role workers during the year, then take back his loan plus interest from the crop. Many sharecroppers were often defrauded by the system). But he would need to get himself and his music together.

Robert decided to leave home and try and locate his real father. He didn't have much to go on, just the name of a town 210 miles to the south from whence his mother had brought him as a baby. However, it was to Hazelhurst, Mississippi (named after the chief engineer of the Illinois central railroad, George H. Hazelhurst) for which Robert headed.

Hazelhurst was to provide a reasonable living for Robert over the next couple of years and also allow him to develop his talents. The rest of the country was deep in depression at that time, but central Mississippi had the WPA building highways for its territory. This meant that there was employment for workers and that they had money to spend on Saturday nights.

Robert's next musical mentor was Ike Zinnerman who was born in Grady, Alabama. Ike apparently told his wife that he had learned to play guitar in a graveyard at midnight while sitting on top of a tombstone. Even in these early times it is interesting to note that musicians were starting to build mythologies about themselves. This was an attempt to gain attention and to separate themselves from the 'common herd'. One day, thousands of miles away in another time, a young white

English guitar player called Eric Clapton would go through a similar myth-building process.

Ike Zinnerman could play the blues, and just as he had done with Son House, Robert attached himself to Ike and learnt all he could. Robert had also re-married by this time to Calletta 'Callie' Craft. They were wed in Copiah County courthouse in May 1931 and kept their marriage a secret; Callie was ten years Robert's senior, had been married twice before and had three small children. She idolised Robert and cooked for him, worked for him and treated him like a king. She also trusted him away from her and didn't worry about him staying out all night at Ike Zinnerman's house.

Robert would often go into the woods on his own and sit and pick the blues. He played the same tune over and over until he got it exactly right. On Saturdays he could be found playing on the public steps of the courthouse and then on Saturday evening's on the familiar circuit of local juke joints.

From the start Robert was not a man to receive much respect in the eyes of those who were labouring with back-breaking work in the fields everyday. He wasn't a big man, he was small and small boned. He had long delicate fingers, wavy hair and a youthful appearance. In the violent juke joints of the time he was not a man who would command much respect. However, he was attractive to women and eventually he learned how to use them, especially older women from whom he came to expect to be mothered and who also invariably gave him somewhere to stay. What respect Robert *did* start to achieve came from his ability as a singer and blues player. Robert Johnson could play anything and he had an uncanny ability to mimic virtually any piece of music he might hear. Years later the same amazing ability to reproduce musical phrases from other blues guitarists was noted by his contemporaries in the young Eric Clapton.

Robert Johnson began to develop a local following around Hazelhurst and was known around those parts as 'R.L.'. He was to tell everyone that asked that the initials stood for Robert Lonnie. 'Lonnie' came from the name of another famous musician, Lonnie Johnson.

However, we should note that Robert's mother had named him Robert Leroy simply because she liked the name Leroy. She had also given the name to her other son, Childs Melvin Leroy Dodds, Robert's older half-brother. However, it was true that Robert Johnson counted Lonnie Johnson among his musical influences and liked the way that he played.

Robert's time in Hazelhurst was to form his personality and it was here that his musical talent began to blossom. However, things went wrong in Robert and Callie's relationship, and Robert eventually deserted her. Callie died a few years later. Robert then returned to Robinsville and it was here that he was to re-encounter Son House and Willie Brown. Apparently one night they were playing at a local juke joint when in walked Robert. They hadn't seen him since the days when he would annoy them by picking up their guitars in musical breaks to try and impress them – all to no avail. So it was with some trepidation that they noticed him walking in with a guitar over his back. He asked them if he could play and after much persistence they gave in. Legend has it that they were totally amazed at his improvement and he was given much praise by both of them. Over the following years Johnson carried on living his nomadic existence until he came across H.C. Speir, who ran a music store in Jacksonville, Mississippi and who had a studio for making records for personal use on the premises. Speir was employed by various record companies as a scout, notably by Paramount Records who recorded a great many of his recommendations. Robert Johnson was keen to record and join an elite of blues performers on record, from many of whom he had learnt his music. Robert had listened extensively to the likes of Leroy Carr, Skip James, Lonnie Johnson and others.

Speir had auditioned Robert Johnson and passed his name on to Ernie Oertle, an ARC (American Record Company) salesman. Oertle decided to take Robert to San Antonio to record. His first session in 1936 was to produce 'Terraplane Blues', which turned out to be his best selling record and a hit for Vocalion Records. He was recalled to Texas in the following June to cut some more tracks. Although this included some of his best work nothing ever sold as well as 'Terraplane Blues'. Vocalion retained six of Johnson's eleven records in their catalogue by December 1938. However, he was never recalled again to record.

Eventually fate was to catch up with Robert Johnson. He had always had an eye for the women and despite repeated warnings by other musicians such as Son House, he thought nothing of flirting with any of the numerous women that would hang around the juke joints egging on the performers.

One Saturday night – 13 August, 1938 – Robert Johnson was playing at the juke house at Three Forks, which was in the Greenwood area. This was a country road house outside of town. As fate would have it Robert had made friends with a local woman, who was the wife of a man that ran the juke joint at Three Forks. Sonny Boy Williamson II was also on the bill that night. As the evening went on, Robert began fraternising with his local lady friend in full view of her husband, a practice he had undertaken many times before. Time passed and more and more alcohol was consumed, but Sonny Boy had noticed that tension was increasing in the house. However, being an experienced performer he was ready.

During a break in the music someone gave Robert a half pint bottle with a broken seal. Sonny Boy knocked it out of his hand and it broke against the ground. He then warned Robert severely never to accept a drink from an already opened bottle since there was no way of knowing whether it had been poisoned or not. However, Robert was angry and retorted: 'Man, don't ever knock a bottle of whisky out of my hand.'

Thus it was that later that same evening, Robert accepted another already opened bottle. This *had* been poisoned – with strychnine – and Robert died on Tuesday 16 August, having contracted pneumonia as an effect of the poisoning. He was later buried in a small grave yard in the Old Zion Church near Morgan City, Mississippi which was very close to Highway 7. He was just twenty-seven years old.

In late 1938, producer John Hammond was looking to recruit musicians for his *Spirituals To Swing* concert, which he intended to stage at Carnegie Hall in New York. He contacted talent scout Don Law in Dallas to ask if he could find Robert Johnson, but Johnson was already dead. In the end John Hammond booked guitarist and songwriter Big Bill Broonzy for the concert.

This is how Eric Clapton describes his discovery of Robert Johnson's music and the effect that it had on him.

'I don't think I'd even heard of Robert Johnson when I first found the record; it was probably fresh out. I was around fifteen or sixteen, and it came as something of a shock to me that there could be anything that powerful. I played it, and it really shook me up because it didn't seem to me that he was particularly interested in being at all palatable; he didn't seem concerned with appeal at all. All the music I'd heard up till that time seemed to be structured in some way for recording. What struck me about the Robert Johnson album was that it seemed like he wasn't playing for an audience at all; it didn't obey the rules of time or harmony or anything – he was just playing for himself. It was almost as if he felt things so acutely he found it almost unbearable. This was an image, really, that I held on to for a very long time.

'At first it was almost too painful, but then after about six months I started listening, and then I didn't listen to anything else. Up until the time I was twenty-five, if you didn't know who Robert Johnson was I wouldn't talk to you. It was almost like that. It was as if I had been prepared to receive Robert Johnson almost like a religious experience that started out with hearing Chuck Berry, then at each stage went further and deeper until I was ready for him. Even then I wasn't quite ready. It was still too powerful, and very frustrating for me, too, because I realised I couldn't play his music any more than I could play Muddy Waters' music. It was just too deep for me to be able to deal with.

'It became, then, a question of finding something that had a

*riff, a form that could be interpreted, simply, in a band format.
The easiest place to start was with the songs where he would
play that Jimmy Reed figure on the bass lines. In 'Crossroads',
there was a very definite riff that came, more or less, from
'Terraplane', actually. He was playing it full-chorded, with the
slide as well. I just took it on a single string or two strings and
embellished it. Out of all of the songs it was the easiest for me to
see as a rock 'n' roll vehicle, but there were certain songs on
the album that I wouldn't touch. They were just too fragile, too
beautiful, to be dissected or arranged. At this stage in my life I
probably wouldn't touch any of them, but back then I had less
inhibition, so I singled out the ones that seemed most accessible
and then I tried to make them even more so to today's market.
So that people would like them, in a sense, on a somewhat
shallow level, and then ask questions afterwards. To have tried
to mimic Robert, vocally or musically, it seemed to me,
wouldn't have made him accessible at all to people that were
listening today. It would have just left the music where it was –
and not as good as what it was either. What I was trying to do
was to draw out the spirit of what was being said as much as
the form or the technique; I was trying to extract as much
emotional content from it as I could, while respecting the form
at the same time.*

*'Robert Johnson to me is the most important blues musician
who ever lived. He was true, absolutely to his own vision, and
as deep as I have gotten into the music over the last thirty years,
I have never found anything more deeply soulful than Robert
Johnson. His music remains the most powerful cry that I think
you can find in the human voice, really. I know when I first
heard it, it called to me in my confusion; it seemed to echo
something that I had always felt.*

*'His best songs have never been covered by anyone else, at
least not very successfully – because how are you going to do
them? In some ways a song like 'Hellhound On My Trail' is*

35

hardly there, it's almost in the air – what he doesn't say, what he doesn't play, it's so light and menacing at the same time. I just think it's time to recognise Robert Johnson for what he was. It would just be great if people could simply appreciate his music for what it is, for its truth and its beauty.'

Chapter 3

Stepping stones

Muddy Waters – Chicago Blues – J.B. Lenoir – Boogie-
Woogie Piano Players – John Mayall

Blind Lemon Jefferson – Blind Willie McTell – Blind Blake –
Blind Boy Fuller – Leadbelly – Cyril Davies

M uddy Waters was born McKinley Morganfield on 14 April, 1915 in Rolling Fork, Mississippi. As with many other blues singers, he started by playing harmonica and didn't take up the guitar until the age of seventeen. Muddy began playing on the now familiar circuit of the juke joints, picnics and parties. At some point early in his career he had heard Son House.

'I had been learning guitar from this Scott Bowhandle. I thought he could play. But then I saw Son House and I realised he couldn't play nothing at all. Son House played this same place for about four weeks

37

in a row, and I was there every night. You couldn't get me out of that corner, listening to what he's doing.'

Muddy Waters had also come into contact with Robert Johnson, but they never met. Muddy Waters describes his own style of blues thus.

> *'I consider myself to be, what you might call a mixture of three. I had part of my own, part of Son House and a little part of Robert Johnson. Robert! No, I seen him at a distance a couple of times, but I never actually seen him to play. I regret that very much, because I liked his style. I thought he was real great from his records. Beautiful. Really though, it was Son House who influenced me to play. I was really behind Son House all the way.'*

Muddy Waters' first recordings were made by Alan Lomax who, along with fellow field researcher John Work, had gone to the Delta to search for Robert Johnson, and who has previously been noted for recording Son House instead for the Library of Congress. On that trip they also recorded Muddy Waters singing and playing with a few of his friends on Stovall's Farms. Alan Lomax was so impressed that he returned the following year and recorded Muddy again.

The experience of being recorded persuaded Muddy to pursue career as a professional musician. Muddy Waters had already started to play and could often be found on 4th Street in Clarksdale playing for money at weekends. However, on one Friday afternoon in May 1943, the twenty-eight year old tractor driver of Stovall's Farms caught the 4 pm train at Clarksville Station and headed for Memphis. He was carrying only his guitar – which he had bought by mail order from Sears & Roebuck from $11 – and a suitcase with one change of clothes. When he arrived in Memphis, Muddy switched trains and boarded the north bound Illinois central to Chicago, which was the end of the line.

Between the end of World War I and the beginning of World War II there had been a mass migration of black workers to the northern industrial cities of the United States. In Chicago they settled on the south side of that great city. With them they brought their music, their religious beliefs, their superstitions and the blues.

When Muddy Waters arrived in Chicago he found a friend in Big Bill Broonzy, who had earlier made his way up from the Mississippi Delta. Through Broonzy, Muddy was to meet Lester Melrose, a white independent record producer. Muddy recorded for Melrose who sold his recordings to Columbia. However, Columbia decided not to release them. By this time Muddy was playing an electric guitar, albeit in the style of a country blues musician. Eventually Sunnyland Slim, another Chicago-based musician, recommended him to Aristocrat, a new Chicago-based label owned by the legendary Chess brothers, Leonard and Phil. Leonard and Phil were Jewish immigrants from Poland who owned several bars in black neighbourhoods – for them, records were strictly a side line. Muddy Waters' first recordings for Chess were 'Gypsy Woman' and 'Little Anna May' and they both proved to be flops. But at least Muddy had some records out in the stores.

Then Chess released 'I Can't Be Satisfied'. Story has it that early one Saturday morning in 1948 the initial pressing of 'I Cant Be Satisfied' was loaded into the trunk of an Aristocrat employee's car and hand-delivered to 180 south-side outlets. By mid-afternoon it was impossible to find a copy and the Chess Brothers were being bombarded with re-orders, which they couldn't supply. Stores that still had copies began to limit sales to one per customer. This was an attempt to prevent Pullman Porters from buying several and re-selling them at a marked-up price on trains and in stations down south. Singles sold for 79 cents in those days, but by the time that day was over 'I Cant Be Satisfied' was selling for twice as much. Muddy, who was driving a truck delivering venetian blinds, didn't have a copy and had to pay $1 and 10 cents for one the following morning. However, the shop-keeper refused to sell him a second copy and he had to send his wife out hoping that should wouldn't be recognised.

Muddy Waters was to record many classic blues including 'Rolling Stone', 'I'm Your Hoochie Coochie Man', 'I Just Want To Make Love to You' and 'Got My Mojo Workin'. However, another of his qualities was his ability as a band leader.

A list of those musicians who passed through Muddy's bands reads like a who's who of Chicago blues greats and includes guitarists Jimmy Rogers, Pat Hare, Luther Tucker and Earl Hooker; harp players Little Walter, Junior Wells, Big Walter Horton, James Cotton and Carey Bell; bass player Willie Dixon; pianists Memphis Slim, Otis Spann and Pinetop Perkins; and drummers Elgin Evans, Fred Below and Francis Clay – many of whom went on to lead their own bands. But of all of these it was only Little Walter who came close to achieving Muddy Waters' success.

Between 1951 and 1960 the Muddy Waters Blues Band was the dominant musical unit in the Chicago area. Muddy Waters was a composer of blues songs, and originals like 'Long Distance Call', 'Manish Boy', 'Got My Mojo Workin', 'She Moves Me' and 'She's Nineteen Years Old' have become blues standards. Muddy also recorded songs that had been given to him by bass player Willie Dixon. 'Hoochie Coochie Man', 'I Just Want To Make Love To You' and 'I'm Ready' have been pounded out in endless bars by white blues bands ever since.

Muddy's records really define the Chicago blues sound. This was a classic period and at the time when the Muddy Waters Blues Band featured Little Walter on harmonica, it is thought by many to have been the finest blues band of all time. Chess Records released Muddy Waters' debut album in 1958. It was called *The Best Of Muddy Waters* and was a collection of his hit singles. In that same year Muddy Waters and his pianist Otis Spann toured England.

However, it was Muddy Waters and his band's performance at the Newport Folk Festival in 1960 that was to have a profound effect on an English blues musician from a working class background. Chess released the live album *Muddy Waters At Newport*, and this album was heard by our English blues musician who up to that point had been an almost snobbish evangelist for country blues. His name was Cyril Davies...

Just after Muddy Waters arrived in Chicago another blues artist appeared on the same scene. His name was J.B. Lenoir. J.B. had arrived via New Orleans where he had worked for a while with Elmore James and harmonica player Sonny Boy Williamson (aka Rice Miller). [Incidentally Sonny Boy Williamson (Rice Miller) is not to be confused with another Sonny Boy Williamson, who was also a harmonica player, and the bracketed inclusion is to distinguish between the two. The other Sonny Boy Williamson met with the traditional violent death in 1948, when he was murdered as he walked home from a club date on Chicago South Side. He was thirty-four. He had recorded for the Bluebird label in the 1930s and '40s and was a fantastic harmonica player. Some of his most famous songs were 'Good Morning Little Schoolgirl', 'Sugar Mama Blues', 'Early In The Morning' and 'Bluebird Blues'. Such was the original Sonny Boy Williamson's stature that Rice Miller, who was himself a great harmonica player, stole his name – a bit of out and out opportunism – and Rice Miller would often be referred to as Sonny Boy Williamson II.]

On arrival in Chicago, Lenoir was befriended – as had been Muddy Waters – by Big Bill Broonzy who helped him to find work in the city's blues club scene. During the fifties Lenoir was to record for Chess, the J.O.B. label and the Parrot label. He returned to Chess on their Checker label in 1955. Lenoir was a popular player in Chicago well into the sixties. However, in 1965 he toured Europe with the American Folk Blues Festival package and he returned again in 1966. These visits gave him a chance to expand his reputation beyond Chicago. Tragically, Lenoir was involved in a serious car accident that year, which caused him to have a fatal heart attack. He was thirty-eight years old.

One of the most interesting things about J.B. Lenoir is that many of his songs departed in their lyrical content from the normal blues themes of love, sex and abandonment. Tunes such as 'Everybody Wants To Know' (about hunger), 'Deep Debt Blues' (about poverty), 'Eisenhower Blues' and 'Korea Blues' were closer to the protest song

41

compositions of the many white folk artists like Bob Dylan and Rambling Jack Elliot from the New York scene of the early sixties. Lenoir sang in a high pitched voice, which was very different to that of Muddy Waters and Son House.

Lenoir was to be a great influence on John Mayall, who recorded a tribute to him called 'The Death Of J.B. Lenoir'.

In a different part of the USA, a different kind of blues had been evolving from that which saw its birth in the Mississippi Delta and which had migrated and transformed itself into the urban blues of Chicago. In Georgia and the Carolinas there were fewer restrictions on black mobility than in Mississippi and consequently there was a greater degree of interplay between black and white culture and their musicians. Along the Atlantic seaboard other names were starting to be heard. Blind Blake, Blind Willie McTell and Blind Boy Fuller were all virtuoso finger-picking guitar players and had a greater grasp of passing chords and rhythmic concepts than their contemporaries from Mississippi.

Blind musicians often came to play because they could not find paying work in any other area. These musicians' lack of sight allowed their hearing capacity to be completely concentrated, which gave them, perhaps, a greater facility to interpret more complex melodies. Blind Lemon Jefferson (*aka* Deacon L.J. Bates) was born July 1897 in Couchman, Texas, and died in December 1929, Chicago, Illinois. Between 1926 and 1929 he recorded almost a hundred titles. He sang everything from religious hymns and spirituals to work songs and folk-tunes. He was truly a songster. But it was through his guitar style that he was to have a lasting effect on his contemporaries and on future blues players.

His single string runs and virtuoso picking gained him a reputation wherever he played. In 1925 Sammy Price, a Dallas piano player and record store employee, recommended Jefferson to Paramount Records. Jefferson's recordings for Paramount were very successful and sold very well. This encouraged Paramount to search for other male blues singer-guitarists. In 1926 they discovered Blind Blake, who along with Blind Lemon Jefferson, were Paramount's biggest selling country blues men of the twenties. Jefferson also recorded for the OKeh label in 1927, and two of the tracks – 'Matchbox Blues' and 'That Black Snake Moan' – were to become his most famous recordings.

Jefferson was another blues musician whose life was to end in tragic circumstances. Legend has it that he died from the effects of a heart attack caused by freezing in a snow storm in Chicago in 1929. No official death certificate has ever been found.

Numerous musicians have been influenced by Jefferson including Blind Willie McTell, Blind Gary Davis, B.B. King and Lightenin' Hopkins.

Blind Blake, born Arthur Phelps in the early 1890s in Jacksonville, Florida, is the epitome – and the original – of this more complex finger-picking line. A stunning musician, he could play virtually anything and his 'Southern Rag' with its double thumb roll is still looked to with wonder by musicians all over the world. At some time during the 1920s Blake went to Chicago, and in 1926 he signed a recording contract with Paramount Records. His first release was 'West Coast Blues', which became a hit and led to a recording career that extended to 1932. Blake was extremely popular and he recorded nearly eighty titles in all. His music was essentially dance music. It could also be looked at as speeded-up ragtime playing, which had been popularised around about the turn of the century by the recordings of Scott Joplin.

Blind Willie McTell was born on 5 May, 1901 in Statesboro, Georgia. He began learning the guitar from his musician mother when he was nine years old. He ran away from home at the age of thirteen and joined a travelling minstrel show, attending schools for the blind in Macon Georgia and then in New York City. Blind Willie McTell was an itinerant musician throughout the thirties and managed to get on record for Columbia in 1929.

Willie McTell played twelve-string guitar and was one of the major stylists of the South East and Piedmont guitar styles of the period. Unlike Charley Patton, Son House and Robert Johnson, McTell had a soft articulate voice. He was never much of a commercial success, but he was a great influence in the folk music revival of the early sixties and his 'Statesboro Blues' became famous at that time. Another classic McTell composition was 'Broke Down Engine Blues'. In 1940 he recorded for John Lomax (father of Alan) and The Library of Congress in Atlanta. When he wasn't recording or travelling, Willie McTell and his long-time associate, fellow blues musician Curly Weaver, could be found playing for tips and spare change on Atlantis Decatur Street – a popular hangout for local blues men. McTell died in 1959.

Another finger picker to obtain notoriety in the 1930s was Blind Boy Fuller who was born Fulton Allen on 10 July, 1907 in Wadesboro, North Carolina. He was so popular that when he died another young guitar picker named Brownie McGhee was rushed into the studio and a record was subsequently released under the name of Blind Boy Fuller No. 2.

The original Fuller was a fantastic finger-picking guitar player who also played bottleneck guitar. He played mostly on North Carolina street corners and in front of tobacco houses in the early 1930s, but he went on to record for the American Record Company and under the direction of producer James Baxter Long his career flourished. Because of Fuller's association with J.B. Long, he was one of the few artists to receive the financial remuneration due to him from royalties.

Fuller is best remembered for tracks such as 'Step It Up And Go' and 'Trucking My Blues Away'. He died in 1941 in Durham, North Carolina from blood poisoning, which was the result of a kidney ailment. He was thirty-two years old.

Born Huddie Ledbetter on 21 January, 1888 at Mooringsport, Louisiana, Leadbelly, one of the most influential of all the American folk blues artists, reputedly earned his nickname as a result of gun shot wounds.

Leadbelly was not really a blues singer in the traditional sense; he was more a songster. In other words he played blues, spirituals and the pop music of the day as well as prison songs, dance tunes and folk-ballet. Leadbelly had come under the influence of the Texas blues man Blind Lemon Jefferson. However, Leadbelly's contribution can be attributed more to his incredible twelve-string guitar playing, plus his compositions which were more folk in orientation. Leadbelly classics such as 'The Midnight Special', 'Rock Island Line', 'Cotton Fields' and 'Bring Me A Little Water Sylvie', as well as 'Good Night Irene', were closer to the music of Woody Guthrie than to the blues. Indeed, in later life Guthrie and Leadbelly were to become major performers on the New York folk scene. However, Leadbelly had definitely led the life of a blues man. He was raised in rural Louisiana to sharecropper parents, and when he left home he wandered through Louisiana and East Texas. Some time around 1915 he met Blind Lemon Jefferson and they worked and travelled with him. Leadbetter was a multi-instrumentalist who could play guitar, mandolin, piano and accordion, but he eventually settled on the twelve-string guitar as the instrument of his choice. He may have first heard the twelve-string played by Mexican musicians who performed in Texas saloons and bordellos. One of the interesting facts to note about Leadbelly's guitar style was his use of the walking bass figure, which was an imitation of the left hand of the barrel house piano players of that time.

Leadbelly was a large man who commanded respect. He had an explosive temper and had many conflicts with the law. In 1917, he killed a man in Texas. He was convicted and sentenced to thirty years in prison at the Huntsvill prison farm. His attempt at escaping resulted in his sentence being increased by another six years. Apparently, he turned out to be a shrewd prisoner and used his musical talent to avoid work details and eventually to obtain a pardon from the Texas Governor, Pat Neff in 1925, having composed a song for him pleading for his freedom.

Leadbelly returned to Louisiana on his release, but in 1930 he was arrested again – this time for assault with intent to murder. Here comes fate once more to play one of its cards. Leadbelly was sent to Angola prison farm in Louisiana where he was discovered in 1933 by John and Alan Lomax. They were at Angola to record folk-songs sung by the prisoners for The Library of Congress. They were immediately struck by Leadbelly's powerful voice and rhythmic guitar style. Also of great use to these field researchers was the fact that Leadbelly had a fantastic knowledge of black folk-songs. The Lomaxes petitioned Louisiana Governor O.K. Allen to pardon Leadbelly, who was set free in 1934. Following his release, he went to work for the Lomaxes as their chauffeur and occasional performer. In 1935, Leadbelly settled in New York City. As well as becoming friends with Woody Guthrie he was also to meet Pete Seeger and blues men Sonny Terry and Brownie McGhee. He was not, however, very successful in the 1930s and '40s, leaving him and his wife on the brink of poverty.

Leadbelly's fame as a tough man became part of the ever growing word-of-mouth grapevine that was to spread across the Atlantic from New York to London, and eventually to Cyril Davies.

Chapter 4

The keyboard players

Clarence 'Pine Top' Smith – Meade 'Lux' Lewis –
Albert Ammons – Pete Johnson – Jimmy Yancey –
Alexis Korner – Geoff Bradford – John Mayall

Boogie-woogie pianists were to have an influential role in the development of the early London blues scene. Both Alexis Korner and Geoff Bradford, as well as John Mayall, had started out learning the keyboards.

Clarence 'Pine Top' Smith was born Clarence Smith on 11 January, 1904 in Troy, Alabama. He was one of the major figures in the development of boogie-woogie piano during the 1920s and his composition 'Pine Top's Boogie' is one of the most influential boogie-woogie piano pieces.

Smith was an influence on virtually every boogie-woogie piano player who followed him. He had taught himself to play the piano and when he was in his teens he began to play at house parties in Birmingham, Alabama.

Eventually he moved to Pittsburgh where he was to work with the legendary Ma Rainey. Smith came to the attention of fellow boogie-woogie pianist Cow Cow Davenport and it was he who suggested that Smith moved to Chicago.

Smith arrived in Chicago in 1928 and ended up living in the same apartment house as fellow boogie-woogie legends Albert Ammons and Meade 'Lux' Lewis. They would often jam together and became good friends.

Pine Top Smith's fame spread throughout Chicago when he started to play at the city's regular house rent parties and on the club circuit. A house rent party was a party that was literally thrown by the owner of the house who charged a small amount for people to attend so that he or she might raise the money to pay the rent. In a sense they were like private clubs and during the 1920s and '30s were a regular fixture of Chicago musical life.

In 1928, Pine Top Smith cut eight sides for the Vocalian Record label, which unfortunately represents his entire recorded legacy. Shortly after these recording sessions Smith was to fall victim to the violence that walked liked a ghost through the black community. While he was playing at an engagement, a fight broke out among the audience. As often happened on these occasions a gun was pulled and shots were fired, and a stray bullet struck Pine Top in the chest and killed him. He was twenty five-years old.

Jimmy Yancey (*aka* Papa Jimmy) was born on 20 February, 1898 in Chicago, Illinois. Yancey was one of the great pioneers of boogie-woogie piano music. His musical style used a repeating bass figure, which is a major part of the boogie-woogie piano technique. Yancey was not quite as fast a player as later performers of this kind of music and he had his own distinctive style and feel. He was also a performer at house rent parties, but he had limited exposure on the club circuit. He was born to a musical family; his father was a Vaudeville entertainer and his brother, Alonzo, was a ragtime pianist. Yancey's career started at an early age when he toured with his father, performing as a tap dancer and singer. It was thus that before he was sixteen he had toured all over America and Europe and had apparently performed for royalty at Buckingham Palace.

During the course of World War I, Vaudeville began to go into decline and on his return to Chicago, Yancey began to look for other ways of expression. He learned the basis of piano from his brother and started to play parties. Despite the fact that he was gaining recognition he did not become a full-time musician. He was a groundskeeper at Comisky Park, home of the Chicago White Sox, and he held on to this job for twenty-five years. He obviously had a love of baseball and had played it at semi-pro level with the Chicago All Americans.

In 1939, Yancey began his recording career and his first recordings were made for the Solo Art label. In addition, he recorded for the Victor, Paramount, Vocalion, Session and Atlantic labels. Some of his better known pieces included 'Yancey Stomp', '35th And Dearborn' and 'State Street Special'. He also recorded with Cripple Clarence Lofton, another legendary boogie-woogie player. Yancey performed at Carnegie Hall in 1948. However, three years later he died of a diabetes-induced stroke at his home in Chicago.

Albert Ammons was born on 23 September, 1907 in Chicago, Illinois. It was Ammons, along with Meade 'Lux' Lewis and Pete Johnson, who was really to popularise the faster boogie-woogie piano style that became so popular in the late 1930s and '40s.

Ammons had been influenced by Jimmy Yancey and Pine Top Smith and his 'Boogie-Woogie Stomp' is based on Pine Top's boogie-woogie. Ammons became a taxi driver in Chicago and eventually he met another taxi driver who was none other than Meade 'Lux' Lewis. Ammons played in Chicago clubs and his first recordings were with his group the Rhythm Kings in 1926.

In 1938, John Hammond was organising his *Spirituals To Swing* concert at Carnegie Hall. This, will you remember, is the same concert for which Hammond was trying – unsuccessfully – to find Robert Johnson, and booked instead Big Bill Broonzy. He also booked Meade 'Lux' Lewis, Albert Ammons and Pete Johnson, the three star boogie-woogie players of the time. According to reports from that era, these three players literally tore the place apart and virtually started a second major craze for the music there and then. They ended up playing the Café Society, a club in Manhattan where the best boogie-woogie could be heard at that time. Meade 'Lux' Lewis' 'Honky Tonk Train Blues' was one of the major inspirations for one of the founder members of the London blues scene – Geoff Bradford.

Chapter 5

Crying the blues... The electric guitar comes of age

T-Bone Walker – Hubert Sumlin – Matt Guitar Murphy –
Willie Johnson – Geoff Bradford – Eric Clapton

T-Bone Walker, born Aaron Thibeaux Walker on 28 May, 1910 in Linden, Texas, is without doubt one of the most influential electric guitar players of all times. He was one of the first blues electric guitar players and has been an influence on virtually everyone including B.B. King, Freddie King, Albert King, Buddy Guy and Otis Rush.

Over the years I have had many conversations with Geoff Bradford about the early days of British blues and about the guitarists and keyboard players that Geoff listened to, and still listens to. So here we have Bradford on T-Bone Walker...

'The point about T-Bone Walker was his tone; the actual sound of his guitar was really beautiful. He used jazzy chording and his lead guitar work was really effective and melodic. His phrasing and his timing were a revelation to me and a massive influence. No one has really bettered him.'

T-Bone Walker really was the first electric blues guitar player to explore the instrument's range of possibilities. He really knew his stuff as far as amplification was concerned and he was able to play in the middle of an orchestra as well as in a small group. Walker was also a really great singer and entertainer. Here we can see a direct link back to Charley Patton; on stage T-Bone Walker would play a guitar behind his back, behind his neck and between his legs. He also would do the splits and twist and gyrate around. He was a really dynamic performer and showman. It is possible to imagine that this legacy of performance influenced Chuck Berry, who in turn was to influence Jimi Hendrix, who was to take stage performance to a new extreme. In passing, it's worth remembering that Jimi Hendrix was, above everything else, actually a blues guitarist himself.

T-Bone Walker learned the basics of blues guitar from the music of Blind Lemon Jefferson and Lightnin' Hopkins. Walker was a master of the shuffle rhythm, which can be heard very much to the fore in the playing of Hopkins, a fellow Texas blues guitar player. Walker moved to the West Coast early in his life, but the spiritual route of his guitar style remains firmly in Texas.

From around 1920 to 1923, Walker led Blind Lemon Jefferson, a friend of the family, around the streets of Dallas. His job was to look after the tin can in which the audience, who were gathered round Jefferson, would place their tips. It was during this time that Walker, not unnaturally inspired by the brilliant Jefferson, began to play the guitar. Since both his parents were musicians, Walker soon became good enough to start travelling. He joined up with the Dr Breeding Medicine Show and played at various carnivals throughout Texas in the mid-1920s.

In 1929, he recorded for Columbia Records under the name of Oak Cliff T-Bone. Oak Cliff was the part of Dallas from which Walker hailed. At this session he cut two songs: 'Wichita Falls Blues' and 'Trinity River Blues'.

Here are some more coincidences and connections...

In 1930, Walker won a Dallas talent contest, the prize being a performance with Cab Calloway's Big Band. Eventually, Walker was to play with other Texas bands, and ended up in California in 1934. One of those bands was the Count Biloski Band and after Walker's departure, a friend of his – one Charlie Christian – took his place. Christian went on to find great fame as the first electric guitar player in jazz.

In 1939, T-Bone Walker joined Les Hite's Cotton Club Orchestra. It was with this organisation that he recorded the track 'T-Bone Blues'. This track is a blues classic and anyone interested in blues lead guitar who hasn't heard it should stop reading this book immediately and go and find a copy.

Because of the success of 'T-Bone Blues', Walker left Hite in 1941 and started his own band. In 1946, T-Bone Walker was in Los Angles where he recorded for the Black & White label. Many of these tracks are also classics including his instrumental 'T-Bone Jumps Again' and his now world famous 'Call It Stormy Monday (But Tuesday Is Just As Bad)'. If you haven't heard '...Stormy Monday' I can only believe you have been living on Mars for most of your life. Walker also cut 'T-Bone Shuffle', another classic.

T-Bone Walker carried on performing until 1974, when he quit after suffering a stroke. In 1975 he died of bronchial pneumonia.

Hubert Sumlin was born 16 November, 1931 in Greenwood, Mississippi, although he was raised in Arkansas, just outside West Memphis. Before taking up the guitar he learned to play the drums. However, it was to the guitar that he eventually turned. He very briefly played with James Cotton before joining the band with whom his playing was to become so influential – the Howlin' Wolf Band. After joining Howlin' Wolf, Sumlin moved to Chicago.

Hubert Sumlin had a guitar sound that was all his own. It was very sharp edged and had great attack. You can hear this sound very well on the Howlin' Wolf classics 'Spoonful', 'I Ain't Superstitious', 'Back Door Man', 'Smokestack Lightnin'' and 'The Red Rooster'.

On one occasion along the way, Sumlin fell out with Howlin' Wolf and joined the Muddy Waters Blues Band for a year, but eventually he rejoined Howlin' Wolf remaining with him until Wolf's death in 1976.

There was a great rivalry between Howlin' Wolf and Muddy Waters on the Chicago scene of the 1950s and although they both respected one another they apparently didn't get along at all.

Matt 'Guitar' Murphy was born 27 December, 1929 in Sunflower, Mississippi and grew up in the Mississippi Delta. By now I am sure it's of absolutely no surprise to you that he should have turned into a great and influential guitar player. He moved to Memphis when he was three years old, where he and brother Floyd eventually began to get a reputation in the blues scene of the 1950s. Matt Murphy was to play guitar with Howlin' Wolf and Junior Parker, with whom he began the Blue Flames band. Brother Floyd was to record with Parker and played on Parker's classic 'Mystery Train'. Eventually, Matt Murphy joined Memphis Slim's band, the House Rockers, and recorded for Vee-Jay and United Artists.

Matt Murphy really is a guitarist's guitarist. In other words he didn't get to become as famous as B.B. King or Robert Johnson. However, he did ironically receive some recognition from the 1980 movie *The Blues Brothers*. His performances on the album *Briefcase Full Of Blues* has brought him much earned recognition.

One of the people on whom he was an influence was Eric Clapton. The other guitarist who was to play with Howlin' Wolf was Willie Johnson, who did not gain even as much recognition as Matt Murphy. [*This Willie Johnson, lead guitarist, is not to be confused with Willie Johnson, Charlie Patton's friend.*] However, for Geoff Bradford, Willie Johnson is also one of the greats.

Chapter 6

Blues falling down like rain...

B.B. King – Freddie King – Elmore James – Buddy Guy –
Eric Clapton – Peter Green – Mick Taylor

B.B. King – born Riley B. King on 16 September, 1925 in Indianola, Mississippi – is without any doubt the most famous black American blues electric lead guitar player of all time. Let's just say that he has influenced everybody and leave it at that because it would take a book the size of a small encyclopedia to cover the whole of his life's work and influence. However, for the record – and for convenience – here are some important facts about B.B. King. He has received awards, honorary degrees, and has been a passionate ambassador for the blues. He has also been one of the art form's greatest popularisers. Many people throughout the world first experienced the blues from hearing a B.B. King record. He is articulate and obviously a spiritual man with great integrity and for this reason he is looked up to by virtually everyone. I do not think I have heard or read a bad word about B.B. King.

King's legendary guitar style is a mixture of the deep country blues of Blind Lemon Jefferson and the urban sophistication of T-Bone

Walker. We should also throw in a dash of Charley Christian, Eddie Lang and Django Reinhardt. However, it is B.B. King's control over his single-string guitar technique that has been so influential. When playing the guitar the use of string bending gives any note played a new dimension of emotion, and B.B. King uses this to great advantage. He also believes in giving the note plenty of space in which to have its emotional effect. This style of playing was to be a major influence on perhaps the greatest European blues lead guitar player of all time, and who was acknowledged by B.B. King as being the only white guitarist to make him 'sweat' – Peter Green.

King's earliest exposure to music came through the church where he learned to sing gospel music. It was also through the church that he started playing guitar, having been taught some basic chords by a minister. From an early age, King was listening to the jazz guitar work of Charlie Christian. Like Muddy Waters before him, he had worked as a farm-hand and tractor driver and played his music at the weekends. B.B. King's cousin Bukka White, another famous blues guitar player, played bottleneck slide guitar in the driving and aggressive style of Son House, who was an obvious musical influence. B.B. King was living with Bukka White in Memphis and eventually returned to the Mississippi Delta in 1946. He stayed there for one more year, then left for good.

In 1947, King moved to Memphis where he came across the legendary harmonica player Sonny Boy Williamson (Rice Miller). It was while Sonny Boy was performing on the West Memphis radio station KWEN that B.B. King plucked up the courage to approach him and ask for work. However Williamson, who auditioned King, found him some work on another Memphis radio station, WDIA. Here, B.B. King would sing and play blues songs for ten minutes every day and also sell an alcohol-based tonic called Pepticon. It's a long way from the sponsorship excesses of today's music scene, but I suppose you could consider this a small step down that road.

In 1949, B.B. King became a disc jockey on WDIA and gave himself the name Beale Street Blues Boy, which, because of its length, was shortened to B.B. (for Blues Boy) – and a legend was born!

B.B. King's time as a disc jockey allowed him to get the very best blues and jazz education by simply listening to the records that he was playing on air. He gained a reputation for his personality as a DJ and started to perform dates in blues clubs. B.B. King was to work with many, many musicians during that time, but notably with Robert Jr Lockwood, with whom he was to learn more complex chords and jazz licks.

King's recording career began in 1949 when he cut four sides for the Bullet label, based in Nashville. However, these early recordings didn't make much impression. In 1951, he recorded for the legendary Sam Phillips at Sun Studios and later at the Memphis YMCA. It was '3 O'clock Blues', recorded at that time, which launched King as a blues star. This track went to No. 1 on the R&B charts and stayed there for seventeen weeks.

Since that time King has recorded prolifically. However, mention should be made of his 1962 album called *Live At The Regal*, which is considered by blues critics to be the greatest blues recording ever made. Indeed, this is classic B.B. King with fantastic vocal performances and lead guitar work full of emotion and attack – and here we reach another of those 'if you haven't heard this record, put down this book, rush out and buy it' moments!

Freddie King (born Freddie Christian on 3 September, 1934 – and no relation to B.B.!) and Buddy Guy (born George Guy on 30 July, 1936) represent a younger generation of blues lead guitar heroes. I will deal with them together since they are both responsible for introducing a far more aggressive form of blues lead guitar playing.

Buddy Guy, along with another great lead guitar player Otis Rush, was much listened to by, and provided inspiration for, Jimi Hendrix. If you don't believe me try listening to Jimi's performance of 'Red House' on his first album and compare it with Otis Rush singing 'Double Trouble' or Buddy Guy singing virtually anything from his repertoire.

Buddy Guy was born and raised in Louisiana and began playing as a professional in Baton Rouge in the early 1950s. However, in 1957 he relocated to – guess where? – Chicago, where he met and was befriended by... yes, it's Muddy Waters again! (I trust events are beginning to form some type of early pattern in your mind by now.)

Having arrived in Chicago and being given the now legendary introduction to the scene by Muddy Waters, Buddy Guy was to beat Magic Sam and Otis Rush in a blues contest called the Battle Of The Blues.

This led to Buddy Guy being recommended to the owner of the

Artistic and Cobra labels, which turned out to be fate playing a not very smart move because having cut two tracks – 'Sit And Cry' and 'This Is The End' – the company went bankrupt.

In 1960, Buddy Guy signed for Chess Records and became a session guitarist playing with artists such as Muddy Waters, Willie Dixon, Little Walter and Sonny Boy Williamson (Rice Miller). In 1962, he made his own record called 'Stone Crazy' which went to No. 12 on the R&B charts. If you compare – and you should do this if you can – Buddy Guy's playing with that of B.B. King and Otis Rush, you will notice the aggression immediately.

On to Freddie King, who is reputed to be a major influence on Eric Clapton's guitar style – and indeed you can hear that influence. However, if I can put this to you in a slightly cheeky way, the previously mentioned Matt 'Guitar' Murphy should also be seriously examined by you guitarists out there in this light. However, let me say here and now that I consider Eric Clapton to be one of the greatest guitarists who ever lived and one of the cruellest things that has ever been said about him is that during his time in the Yardbirds, John Mayall's Bluesbreakers and Cream, Clapton was simply recycling the blues riffs of all of these aforementioned guitar greats.

Now, we all have to start somewhere and unless you haven't been paying attention to the story so far, you cannot escape from the conclusion that everyone influenced everyone else. The point is it's what you do with these influences that really counts. I consider this cheap jibe that was made against Eric Clapton to be factious and bordering on ignorant and I really wish people would stop making it.

Listen, if you can, to all the electric guitar players listed above and you will be listening to the greatest performances of electric lead guitar playing. But if you are really honest, you will realise when you listen to Eric Clapton performing in John Mayall's Bluesbreakers that he had a sound, a timing and phrasing which were all his own.

So back to Freddie King...

Freddie was born and raised in Texas, but he came of age as a musician in Chicago. As he was growing up he was listening to those legendary country blues guitarists, Blind Lemon Jefferson, Lightnin' Hopkins and Arthur 'Big Boy' Crudup.

And now for another aside: the first track recorded by the young

Elvis Presley was an Arthur 'Big Boy' Crudup composition, called
'That's Alright (Mama)'.

Back to the plot...

After Freddie King and his family had moved back to Chicago in
1950 (the year that I was born), King began the normal circuit of
attending the blues clubs and watching the likes of Muddy Waters and
Jimmy Rogers. He first recorded in the 1950s for El-Bee, a very obscure
label, and he also did a few sessions for the Chess label. However, it
wasn't until he signed for Federal Records in 1960 that he began to
attract attention. He came under the influence of Sonny Thompson,
the A&R man for King Records (Federal was a subsidiary of King
Records). Freddie recorded 'Lonesome Whistle Blues' and 'I'm Tore
Down' and he also recorded the classic 'Have You Ever Loved A
Woman', which was written by Bill Myles. Eric Clapton in his later
career has recorded both 'Have You Ever Loved a Woman' (with Derek
& the Dominos) and more recently 'I'm Tore Down' on his recent blues
album *From The Cradle*.

Freddie King also recorded a number of guitar instrumentals in the
early sixties, two of which – 'Hideaway' and 'The Stumble' – were
recorded by Eric Clapton and Peter Green. (Eric Clapton did 'Hide
Away' and Peter Green did 'The Stumble', both while they were in John
Mayall's Bluesbreakers.)

King went on to have a successful career in the sixties and the early
seventies. However, he died aged forty-two in 1976 of bleeding ulcers
and heart failure.

Elmore James, born Elmore Brooks 27 January, 1918 in Richland,
Mississippi, is included here because of his obvious influence on both
Eric Clapton and Peter Green. He was also an influence on Duane
Allman and Johnny Winter. Elmore James was himself heavily
influenced by the playing of Robert Johnson who, as you will
remember, was influenced by Son House and Charley Patton.

James is world-famous for his slide guitar playing and for original
songs such as 'Shake Your Money Maker' and 'Done Somebody Wrong'.
He was also a fantastic performer of slow blues. You can hear this best
in his performances of Tampa Red's 'It Hurts Me Too' and of his own
'The Sky Is Crying'. One of Robert Johnson's songs is a track called
'I Believe I'll Dust My Broom'. Elmore James was to record his own

version of this track, which he called 'Dust My Broom' and this, along with the distinctive guitar riff he used to accompany the track, is probably his most famous piece. He was also a fine singer and his voice was able to convey great emotion. It almost sounded haunted and any of his slow blues tracks would make a fitting soundtrack to that 'I sold my soul to the Devil at the crossroads' myth we touched on earlier in this book.

So now we have the background to the British blues movement. American blues was its source and also, for virtually all its performers, its passion.

I would like now to put a very important idea in to your minds, and that is this: although almost all of the performers on the London blues scene had to some extent studied American blues music, the new young audience that was attracted to the scene was virtually ignorant of any of the above influences outlined in previous chapters of this book. You have probably heard the legend of how, during Eric Clapton's stint as lead guitarist in the Yardbirds, and subsequently in John Mayall's Bluesbreakers, writing began to appear on walls in London stating 'Clapton is God'. What these meant was that he was a God-like lead guitar player. Consider this: most of this new audience had never heard any blues records in their life – or at least very few. I think, therefore, this goes some way to explaining the impact of Eric Clapton on his audience as he started to create what, for him, was playing that would echo the Chicago sound.

What every great lead guitarist needs is a great rhythm section (bass guitar, drums plus keyboards or rhythm guitar). Eric Clapton found this rhythm section with John Mayall. Now John Mayall was, and is, a great band leader in the tradition of Muddy Waters. And what every great band leader needs is a club scene to play in. He needs to get gigs.

This leads us on to our consideration of the London blues scene created by Cyril Davies, Alexis Korner and Geoff Bradford. It was into this scene that John Mayall was invited by Alexis Korner, who fulfilled the role that Muddy Waters and Big Bill Broonzy had performed to new arrivals on the Chicago blues scene. Alexis was the catalyst. He was the man, and he could introduce you to the right people on the London scene just as Broonzy and Waters could in Chicago.

Chapter 7

An American dream

Picture this! I'm sure it's an image that you see many times. You are at the cinema and an advert comes on the screen before the main feature or perhaps you are watching television and a similar advert appears. It's the USA, it's a desert town, it's the outskirts of a dessert town, an open-top car cruises slowly out of town on a highway. In the car there's a guy, a girl, they both look fit, they both have beautiful bodies and more than anything else they look 'cool'. The advert now proceeds to sell you some beer or jeans or a laptop computer or a mobile phone and on and on and on... The music that accompanies these images in recent times has invariably been either vintage blues or someone playing instrumental slide guitar in the manner of Ry Cooder's soundtrack for the movie *Paris Texas*.

Or perhaps our hero is sitting in the carriage of a train, which is threading its way through a dramatic rocky landscape; the sun is streaming through the carriage window and the hero, of course, is drinking the right kind of beer. In the background we hear Howlin'

Wolf singing 'Smokestack Lightenin'.

Or how about this one? A large deserted room – could be a loft space in New York or Chicago. The sun streams through the windows, the atmosphere is slightly smokey. Into the scene moves an old black man. At first sight he could be a janitor. The music strikes up and he proceeds to dance a solitary tap routine, then once again we are encouraged to buy that beer.

The whole point about all of this is that it's 'cool'.

If you were looking around for a scene or a situation, or a time and a place that was the complete opposite of these images, then London in the late fifties and early sixties would fit the bill nicely. What we are looking at here is 'uncool' big time.

For many young people growing up in fifties' England, the worst thing about their lives was that they were not American. Following the war, many areas of Europe were just one big field of rubble. Germany was decimated and English cities had suffered heavy bombardment. In fact, despite its victory, Britain was virtually bankrupt at the end of 1945.

America, on the other hand, was on the up and up. War industries had pulled the country out of the depression. There was plenty of work for all and, being the victors, America had now become the most powerful nation on earth. They had exploded the atom bomb. They were the 'big boy' in the playground with the big stick.

The fifties saw for most American families technological advances that for the first time were entering the home: washing machines, spin dryers, refrigerators and televisions were all beginning to arrive on the scene, and a new generation was growing up with full employment and a genuine feeling of optimism about the future.

With every new generation comes the potential of a new music; for the American youth in the fifties it was rock 'n' roll. The blues, or a speeded-up electrified version of it, became known as R&B (rhythm and blues). A new generation of black players began to emerge such as

Chuck Berry, Little Richard and James Brown to mention just a few. However, perhaps the crucial moment was when a young American white boy called Elvis Presley, recorded Arthur 'Big Boy' Crudup's 'That's Alright (Mama)', which was released on the Sun record label in 1954. Life would never be the same again.

American rock 'n' roll and American consumer culture hit England during the fifties. By that time things were beginning to look up and the economy was slowly recovering. Food rationing, which had been in force during the war years, was finally abolished during the early fifties and there was full employment. Conscription in England was still in force, which meant that you had to fulfil your national service by joining one of the Armed Forces. However, by the end of the fifties this had been abolished.

In London, coffee bars with juke boxes in the corner containing all the latest American hits, began to spring up everywhere. Bill Haley & The Comets recorded 'Rock Around The Clock' and 'Shake Rock 'n' Roll', the latter reaching No. 4 in the charts in the UK in 1954. The response from the youth of England was to produce a whole load of American imitations. Cliff Richard was obviously an Elvis clone.

In England, and especially in London, the consumer boom eventually began to take hold. Black and white televisions started to appear increasingly in working class households as did washing machines, spin dryers and so on... And then there was the radio, which had been part of English culture in a big way since the thirties and all through the war years. It is important to remember this point about radio, since it was the major mass communication medium. The BBC dominated the airwaves and despite being able to pick up the occasional exotic sound from other parts of the world if you tuned into short wave, as far as the majority were concerned it was the BBC – or nothing at all!

Now we must examine a minority interest that was to provide the seeds of the London blues scene, which was to give John Mayall and his future Bluesbreakers that all-important exposure. The minority interest we are talking about is the trad jazz scene. New Orleans jazz had become a passion for a number of enthusiastic jazz players who had been in the Forces during the war and were now home free. Two of these enthusiasts were jazzman Ken Colyer and trombonist Chris Barber. In 1952, a banjo player who was born Anthony James Donnegan on 29 April, 1931 in Glasgow, joined Ken Colyer's Jazzmen as a guitar and banjo player.

In that band Donnegan was re-united with his old Army friend Chris Barber. Some time earlier, Donnegan was playing on the same bill as the US blues guitarist, Lonnie Johnson. A confused MC got mixed up as to who he was about to announce and introduced Donnegan not as James but as Lonnie – and the name stuck.

Lonnie Donnegan had an interest in blues and folk and this was to earn him a solo spot on the *Ken Colyer Jazzmen's Show*. This rapidly developed into a small group – a band within a band – with Ken Colyer on guitar, Barber on bass and Bill Colyer on washboard. They began to sing US blues and work songs and this music was given the name 'skiffle'. In 1953, some of Donnegan's skiffle numbers were recorded on a session he did with Colyer's band, but nothing happened to these tracks – that is, they were never released at this time.

In January 1954, Chris Barber split from the Ken Colyer's Jazzmen, taking with him many musicians, including Lonnie Donnegan. Barber subsequently formed the Chris Barber Jazz Band and signed to Decca. The band was dedicated to performing traditional New Orleans jazz – hence the term 'trad jazz'. Many other trad jazz bands emerged and this music was to dominate the London club scene from the mid-fifties through to the early sixties.

In 1955, the Chris Barber Jazz Band released a ten-inch album called *New Orleans Joy*, which contained two tracks credited to Lonnie Donnegan's Skiffle Group. These were 'The Rock Island Line' and 'John Henry'. Lonnie Donnegan had learned 'Rock Island Line' from the playing of Leadbelly – remember him? Amazing how this all begins to fit together like some vast, but very improbable jigsaw puzzle. 'Rock Island Line' was an unexpected UK hit reaching No. 8 and spending twenty-two weeks in the charts.

Here's another little throwback to those earlier blues times. Lonnie Donnegan never received any royalties from his hit, having been paid a £50 session fee when it was recorded. Donnegan signed to Pye-Nixa in the UK as a solo performer. On 21 April, 1956, 'Rock Island Line' made No. 8 in the US charts, which took overall sales to over a million. On 19 May, Lonnie Donnegan made his US television debut on the *Perry Como Show* alongside Ronald Reagan, who was appearing in some comedy sketches. Donnegan's band was a trio comprising stand-up bass and drums with Denny Wright on electric guitar.

They set off on an US tour for a month and somewhat ironically for Donnegan, who you will remember is a Scotsman, he was billed as the Irish Hillbilly. In June 1956, his first release on the Pye record label – 'Lost John' – hit No. 2 in the UK charts and made it to No. 58 in the US charts. This was quickly followed in July by the release of his first EP (extended play, which was like a small album containing four tracks) called 'Skiffle Session'. This went to No. 20 in the UK charts. In September, significantly Lonnie Donnegan was to record and release another Leadbelly classic – 'Bring A Little Water Sylvie'. Donnegan went on to have many, many more hits throughout the fifties and into the sixties.

In the UK the skiffle boom was on. Literally hundreds and hundreds of young men raced out to buy guitars, washboards and so on, and since most of them would have been unable to afford a double bass there emerged a substitute instrument called a tea-chest bass, which was made at home using a simple set-up. This was achieved by tying one end of a chord to the top of a broom handle, then anchoring the other end of the chord to the tea chest, putting some tension into the chord by resting the broom handle on the tea chest so you could get bass notes. When I was growing up in the fifties I well remember one of our neighbours in our block of flats in Battersea being part of a skiffle band and actually playing a tea-chest bass right in front of me on many occasions.

Chapter 8

The guv'nor

Alexis Korner was born in Paris, France on 19 April, 1928. He was the child of an Austrian Army cavalry officer and a Greco–Turkish mother. In his early years, Alexis was a much travelled child, living with relatives in many places in continental Europe while his father tried various different business activities, including drilling for oil in Abyssinia. Korner's schooling took place in North Africa, Switzerland, France and England. The family settled in England in the mid-1930s.

Not surprisingly after all this disruption, Alexis turned out to be a very difficult child. He ended up in Finchden Manor School, which was for extremely disturbed boys with a high IQ. It was while he was attending this school that Korner became interested in the guitar. His father did not approve, but Alexis persevered and actually made his own instrument from plywood and a shaved-down table leg.

His family approved of classical music and, along with many other parents of their generation, were rather against the music of a popular orientation. So what we have here is Alexis Korner: a rebel with a cause.

His father was hoping that he would join him in business. Unfortunately for his father, this was not to be.

In the 1940s, Alexis heard a Jimmy Yancey record called 'The Five O'clock Blues'. When I met Alexis much later on, he told me that from that moment onwards that's what he wanted to play. As Korner grew through his teenage years he began to develop a love for jazz. Eventually, he had to fulfil his national service duties and was drafted into the Army in 1946 and sent to Germany. (Incidentally, John Mayall also ended up in the Army and served some time in Korea.) This tour of duty was to prove a significant event in Korner's life for non-military reasons.

While based in Germany, Alexis ran a record library and arranged jazz broadcasts for the British Forces Network. In 1947, he returned to England and found work as an A&R man (artist and repertoire) with a company called Melo Disc Records; following that he got a job as a publicist with Decca Records and also became a studio manager for the BBC.

In his spare time he began to play in small amateur groups, gaining his first professional job with the Chris Barber Jazz Band in 1949. Because of his love for boogie-woogie music, Korner had learned the piano. He later told me...

'My biggest musical fantasy in my younger years and one which I still retain to this day would be this... A young man walks into a party. All the right people are there. It's late at night and after hours. There's a piano in the corner. The young man nonchalantly strolls over to the piano and sits down. He starts to tinkle the keys and when he eventually has everyone's attention he plays a storming boogie-woogie piano piece, gets up and walks out of the room, never to be seen again.'

Thinking about it now, this kind of reminds me of the Clint Eastwood western character, 'The man with no name', who arrives in town out of nowhere, sorts out the bad guys and leaves, usually having bedded at least one rebellious female spirit in the course of the action.

It also reminds me of that story about Robert Johnson from earlier in the book, when he returned seemingly from nowhere to take musical revenge on his musical taunters Son House and Willie Brown. This fantasy is a peculiar masculine cliché and to some extent secretly I think it was shared by both Eric Clapton and Peter Green.

Having begun as a pianist, Alexis Korner started to perform on guitar and built up to appearing three nights a week for five shillings a night. (In old English currency, that wasn't bad; but we are not talking 'big time' here.) In 1948, Alexis Korner tried for the first time to form his own band with a trumpeter called Dickie Hawdon. However, he immediately ran into serious problems because British audiences weren't prepared for the modern jazz that his group was trying to play. In 1950 the band split up.

Luckily for Alexis he had a very good day job and for the rest of the fifties and beyond, he was able to earn a living by working as a journalist and radio announcer. However, privately he still retained a burning aspiration to make it as a successful musician. In 1952, Alexis returned to a band which was led by Chris Barber. This group featured Ken Colyer, who had just come back from playing jazz in New Orleans for a time. Within this group, as we have previously seen, was the young Lonnie Donnegan. In due course, from Korner's point of view he began to disagree with the musical direction. Korner subsequently left the band, and ended up playing in a London club in Greek Street.

Having made the long journey from the Mississippi Delta through the Chicago blues scene, across the Atlantic, into this palace of 'uncool' London in the mid-fifties, we now reach a seminal moment which, at the time, appeared no more important for Alexis Korner than many other moments in which he was to meet musicians. In the mid-fifties, Alexis Korner met a young British blues harmonica player called Cyril Davies and they started to play together at local clubs.

Cyril Davies was born in England in 1932. He had been interested in jazz and blues in his teens, had played banjo in several jazz bands in the early fifties and was hooked by the skiffle craze. This was to be very important for Cyril Davies since you will remember that our skiffle hero, Lonnie Donnegan, was to record a number of Leadbelly compositions. It was through these records that Cyril Davies discovered the music of Leadbelly and began to hear more and more blues.

Now as a man, Cyril Davies was of the same type as Charley Patton, Son House and Leadbelly – that is, he was a tough guy. His day job was as a panel beater (an English term to describe somebody who fixes dents in car bodies that result from accidents). It is a very skilled job and carried with it in those days, and even today, some status. Cyril Davies discovered the music of Little Walter, who you will remember was a harmonica player in the great Muddy Waters blues band and subsequently went on to have his own solo career. Cyril Davies was very impressed by the harmonica sound Little Walter was obtaining through his use of a microphone and amplifier. Little Walter would cup his hands around his harmonica and a microphone, and by doing so was able to create extremely emotional and expressive lead lines.

At this point it is worth noting that the harmonica was being used in the Muddy Waters Blues Band in a similar way to the use of electric guitar as a lead instrument.

According to Geoff Bradford, Cyril Davies met Alexis Korner at the Round House pub in Wardour Street in London's West End. Cyril had been running a skiffle club with not much success, and Alexis Korner suggested that they team up together and, significantly, form a rhythm and blues club. What had happened here was that having worked their way through skiffle in Davies' case, and jazz in Alexis Korner's case, they had both searched for the source of this music – which was, of course, in both their minds the blues.

It's perhaps worth noting that many modern scholars consider the blues to have evolved on a separate line to jazz, but if you talk to enough jazz players they will all tell you that blues is the root.

Anyway, Korner and Davies formed their new rhythm and blues club and gave it the name England's Firstest And Bestest Skiffle Club on 1 September, 1955. In March 1957, they changed the name to The

London Blues & Barrelhouse Club. (A barrelhouse is another name for our old friend the juke joint, and the word 'barrelhouse' was actually used as a verb – that is, you went 'barrelhousing'; you know, you got drunk, hung out with the wrong type of women, in other words you had a load of fun.)

The club was an immediate success with fellow musicians. However, it didn't exactly draw in the crowds. During this period Korner and Davies presented such guests as Muddy Waters, Sonny and Brownie McGhee and Memphis Slim. Musicians would just drop in if they happened to be in town. Another incredible influential musician who played there on a regular basis was folk guitar legend Davy Graham.

One musician who was attracted to the club was a brilliant piano player called Keith Scott, who became a kind of semi-resident, playing boogie-woogie piano à la Meade 'Lux' Lewis and Pine Top Smith on a regular basis. Meanwhile another young musician had returned home fresh out of the Navy. His name was Geoff Bradford.

Geoff had taught himself to play guitar while in the Navy, having got his first guitar in Sicily.

'I had heard Bo Diddley on AFM [American Forces Network] and I also saw Big Bill Broonzy on British TV. That's the famous piece of footage of Broonzy playing in the basement of a Paris club. It was all dark and atmospheric with smoke rising; very romantic.'

Geoff had been in the Mediterranean fleet and spent his time cruising up and down the Mediterranean. He had formed a little skiffle group while still on the boat. Originally, Geoff had had piano lessons and at a very early age became interested in the music of the great boogie-woogie players – notably 'Honky Tonk Train Blues', that Meade 'Lux' Lewis classic. Not long after Geoff returned to civilian life, he decided he needed to find some other musicians to play with and placed an advert in a music publication called *Melody Maker*. (The publication had a Musicians Wanted section where you could advertise to meet other musicians who shared your interests.) One of the first musicians to reply to Geoff's advert was Keith Scott, who turned out to have an extensive record collection.

The early London rhythm and blues scene had developed into a kind of secret society. At that time records were hard to get, especially from America. There were a number of specialist shops, notably Dobells in Charing Cross Road. Geoff remembers many a trip down to Dobells where he and his mates would cram into the tiny listening booth, all smoking and listening to the latest blues, or rhythm and blues, releases from America. To meet someone who had an extensive collection of his own was like winning the lottery. (Slight time jump forward: John Mayall who was growing up in Manchester at this time, inherited a large collection from his father – more interlinked coincidences...)

Having formed a friendship with Keith Scott, Geoff Bradford was taken by Keith to the Round House in Wardour Street. It was here that Bradford met up with Cyril Davies and Alexis Korner and became a regular part of the Round House scene. By this time Geoff was playing a national steel resonator guitar which in no small way helped to spread his fame, because no one else on the scene had one.

As a guitar player, Geoff Bradford was in a class of his own, according to all accounts of that time. Cyril Davies by that time had a twelve-string guitar and was reproducing the music of Leadbelly as well as he could. Cyril was a fine singer and twelve-string guitar player. Alexis was playing basic lead guitar on acoustic guitar behind Cyril Davies' twelve-string playing and from time to time Cyril would also play the harmonica, an instrument on which he had become very proficient. No one had ever seen anything like Geoff Bradford's playing, though, and he began rapidly to gain a reputation.

Geoff Bradford is a very quiet and unassuming man and remains so even to this day. He remembers...

'On many occasions Alexis would disappear from the Round

House for long periods of time and that's how I ended up
beginning to play guitar with Cyril Davies.'

Up until that time Bradford and Scott had been recreating the music of
two American black blues players called Scrapper Blackwell and Leroy
Carr, who had released a number of more sophisticated urban blues
duets between 1928 and 1935, the year that Carr died (aged thirty).
Among the tracks that they recorded for the Vocalian label were the
classic 'How Long Blues', 'Blues Before Sunrise', 'Mean Mistreater
Mama' and 'Prison Bound'. Leroy Carr was a heavy drinker and his
death was caused by acute alcoholism.

During this period Cyril Davies and Alexis Korner worked together
as session musicians. They both backed Chris Barber's wife Ottlie
Patterson on R&B sessions, which became a feature of the Chris Barber
band. The Patterson/Korner/Davies session would normally end the
set. It was during these sessions that Korner and Cyril Davies started
using amplified instruments.

Now this switch to amplification would not seem like any big deal
to us musicians in modern times, but in a weird hang-up of the times,
switching from acoustic to electric instrumentation was considered by
many so-called blues purists to be a form of heresy. Many local
musicians on the scene at the time were to turn on Alexis Korner and
Cyril Davies as if they had sold out. It's worth noting that this fate was
to await Bob Dylan when he toured Europe in the sixties with the
Band. He himself was accused of selling out. This whole thing needs to
be seen as a strange form of musical snobbery, which is very difficult for
us to understand today, but was very real at the time.

Eventually Alexis Korner and Cyril Davies had had enough of trying
to run the Round House, and it duly closed. Meanwhile, Davies had
started to hear records by the great Muddy Waters blues band and as
Geoff Bradford recalls:

'As soon as Cyril heard that, he decided he must switch on a full
time basis to an electric band format.'

Cyril Davies and Alexis Korner had drifted apart, but they were to come together again in February/March 1962 when they decided to open up what was to become the first proper blues club in Britain. The club met on a Saturday night, opening on 17 March, 1962 (St Patrick's Day) in a basement, which was reached by going down some steps between the ABC tea shop and the jewellers across the road from Ealing Broadway train station.

Alexis Korner later recalled for me that fatal day:

'I thought we were going to get killed since not far away was a pub full of drunken Irishmen celebrating St Patrick's Day. However, we got going and from the start we were an instant success.'

Cyril Davies and Alexis Korner, as you will remember, had already been performing impromptu gigs with the Chris Barber band, but they couldn't find any other work for their new electric R&B set up because club promoters and owners were not interested in such untried music. This led directly to the opening of their new club to which they gave the name the Ealing Club.

It was at this club that Korner and Davies started to play as Blues Incorporated. A loose group of musicians formed this band and the line up would change on a regular basis; at various times the group included Long John Baldry on vocals, Dick Heckstall-Smith on saxophone, Charlie Watts on drums, Alexis Korner on guitar and vocals, Cyril Davies on vocals and harmonica, Art Woods (brother of the current Rolling Stones' guitar player, Ronnie Wood) on vocals, Andy Hoogenboon on bass and Keith Scott on piano.

Another young blues enthusiast who arrived very early at the Ealing Club was Mick Jagger, who was at that time studying at the London School of Economics. Mick first attended the Ealing Club on 24 March, 1962 after reading about it in *Melody Maker*.

'We went on the tube, and that was our first encounter with Alexis. It wasn't the kind of rhythm and blues that we had expected or liked to play ourselves. It was more of a jazz band in our opinion. Alexis though, he was a great band leader but he wasn't much of a vocalist. He used to sit on a stool playing an acoustic guitar with a pick up across the sound hole. Then he would start singing his funny blues interpretations in what seemed to us like a very upper class English accent. We all used to hoot with laughter about this.

'Cyril Davies played very good harmonica and I had never seen anyone play it like that before and, of course, Charlie Watts was playing the drums. I saw people my own age getting up to sing and play – people like Paul Jones and Brian Jones – and I thought to myself, "they aren't that brilliant, I can do as well as that". So I got up and I sang 'I Got My Mojo Working' and before I knew what was happening I was one of the band's featured vocalists. Then Keith Richards would come up and we would do a couple of Chuck Berry things. That's how it all started.'

The day 3 May, 1962 was to be another key moment in the assault of R&B music on the London music scene, which up until very recently had been dominated by the trad jazz movement. One of the strongholds of the trad jazz crowd was a club called the Marquee, but on that fateful Thursday evening, Blues Incorporated began a residency. Alexis Korner later told me:

Thursday evening was a dead night, a musicians' graveyard; and we were warned by everyone about taking it on. But it took off and very soon it was wall to wall stuff.'

Very shortly after this Blues Incorporated began to get gigs in other venues, some of which were out of town. One of these was a club called the Twisted Wheel in Manchester. Alexis and Cyril and their band played here on many occasions and it was here that a musician in his late twenties was to see them play. This musician was John Mayall.

The friendship that he formed with Alexis Korner was, in 1963, to lead the twenty-nine year old John Mayall in to taking a life-changing decision. However, more of this later!

Meanwhile, back in London an R&B fan from Cheltenham, a provincial town in the south of England, started to travel to the Ealing club and the Marquee. He began to play under the pseudonym of Elmo Lewis. His talent was to play slide guitar and he had been inspired by our famous trio of Son House, Robert Johnson and Elmore James. His real name was Brian Jones, and he looked more like a choirboy than a blues player. Alexis Korner remembered:

'Brian used to turn up at my house at odd times and I would put him up. He would listen to my record collection. It was a kind of education. It would be Howlin' Wolf one week and Elmore James the next. He always had a list of who he wanted to hear.'

One thing I can tell you from my friendship with Alexis Korner, which came along much later: he was a very charming man and very generous in his advice. He was always ready to help you to extend your knowledge of the London blues scene or American blues and jazz in general.

I first met Alexis Korner because he came and played sessions on the Capital Radio programme I had been putting together in the early seventies. Early on during that period I was given the opportunity by Alan Bates, who owned the Black Lion jazz label, to produce my first album. This was a Geoff Bradford solo blues record and I remember proudly taking it round to Alexis Korner's London office – at that time based in Chiswick High Road, just across the river from Richmond, Surrey, which was my home.

Alexis sat down and played the whole album and was very complimentary about my production. I was so nervous; this was my first record production and there I was playing it in front of one of the men that had started the whole London blues scene, but what I got from Alexis was nothing but support. This was totally typical of the man.

Going back to Brian Jones, it's worth noting that not long after this both Eric Clapton and Peter Green were to receive a similar addition to their musical education from John Mayall, who made his record and tape collection available to the young guitarists as well as providing accommodation at his house. Now Brian Jones was of a younger generation to Mayall, Davies and Korner, but he was already a good slide guitarist. He was inspired to form his own group.

During April and May of 1962, Geoff Bradford was in an interval group (a group that literally played in the interval between the two sets performed by the main band at a gig). Geoff's group featured Andy Wren on piano and vocal, Ernie Rogers on bass and Bob Wackett on drums, with Geoff on electric lead guitar. Like many other musicians, Geoff had made the jump to playing the electric guitar. He told me:

'I just went out and got myself an electric. It was a twin pick up Supro electric. Lots of people were playing electric guitar with a pick. You have to remember there had been the big Shadows thing with Hank Marvin and also the twangy guitar sounds of Duane Eddy. [Hank Marvin was one of the influences on the guitar sound of Peter Green.] I couldn't play with a pick because it kept falling out of my hand so I decided to finger-pick the electric guitar.'

Geoff's interval band was playing for Blues Incorporated at the Marquee. Geoff remembers:

'We had just finished our interval set when this young guy came straight up to the bandstand and approached me and asked me if I would like to join a rehearsal band he was putting together. He said: "My band's going to be really big. It's going to be the greatest." I thought, "why not!". Brian Jones' new band started to rehearse at the White Bear pub in Lisle Street with a different bass player and drummer turning up every

time. Andy Wrenn just didn't seem to fit in so I invited another
singer that I knew called Brian Knight.'

Now Brian Knight was a prodigy of Cyril Davies. He worked with Cyril
at the same panel beating car repair business and became Cyril Davies'
unofficial chauffeur (shades of Leadbelly driving Alan Lomax around).
Brian Knight had already gained a reputation as a harmonica player and
so he began to attend rehearsals. The personnel kept changing.
Keyboard player Ian Stewart had joined on piano; he was another
boogie-woogie fanatic.

However, Brian Jones was about to make that error with Geoff
Bradford that you will remember from the beginning of our book. One
day he brought Keith Richards in and they started trying to play Chuck
Berry numbers. Brian Knight had no intention of singing Chuck Berry
and, as you will remember, Geoff Bradford had no intention of playing
Chuck Berry – and both Bradford and Knight left.

So, oh dear me! No vocalist for Brian Jones' new band. Keith
Richards suggested his old friend Mick Jagger. You will remember that
the two of them had already been jumping up and doing the odd
Chuck Berry number at the Ealing club. Jagger came down and things
started to gel – and they decided to choose a name for the band. They
chose the name the Rolling Stones after one of Muddy Waters' most
famous recordings. The early Rolling Stones started out performing the
music of Elmore James, Jimmy Read, John Lee Hooker and Chuck Berry.

Brian Knight and Geoff Bradford went on to form their own band
in June 1962, called the Blues By Six. This band featured Geoff on
guitar, Geoff's old buddy Keith Scott on piano, Art Themen on
saxophone, Dave Gelly also on saxophone, Andy Hoogenboon on bass
and a jazz drummer called Charlie Watts. Eventually, Charlie decided
that he couldn't carry on with the Blues By Six. The reason he couldn't
cope, Brian Knight told me years later, was that he had a good day job
at an advertising agency, which he was reluctant to leave.

The Blues By Six often managed more than nine gigs a week,
though they were all holding down day jobs at this time. They would
get to gigs in Brian Knight's dad's Ford Anglia and in Charlie Watts'

dad's Humber. Eventually they ended up with a Bedford Dormer. Anyway, Charlie Watts left to join a band with fewer gigs, as playing the drums was just his spare-time recreation. The band with the fewer gigs, of course, turned out to be the Rolling Stones. Charlie Watts was replaced on drums by Del Manfredi.

The Blues By Six was a fantastic blues band and literally tore the life out of numbers by Muddy Waters, Howlin' Wolf, John Lee Hooker and so on. However, Geoff Bradford was eventually to become reunited with Cyril Davies. Alexis Korner recalled:

'Eventually, me and Cyril fell out over musical differences again. I was more into the jazz thing and by that time Jack Bruce and Ginger Baker, as well as Dick Heckstall Smith and Graham Bond had started to turn up. Cyril wanted to go in the direction of Chicago blues and I wanted to get more jazz in. He saw no place for saxophone in the band and he also wanted Ginger Baker out. They just didn't see eye to eye, so Cyril and I split up and split up very thoroughly. He just up and left and it turned into a little bit of rivalry between us. Before this happened, record producer Jack Good, sold the First Blues Incorporated Marquee gig and produced an R&B album from the Marquee which came out in 1962. However, it came out on the Decca Records budget label, Ace of Clubs, for some unfathomable reason.'

So Cyril Davies split and formed his own band called the Cyril Davies R&B Allstars. Cyril took over the personnel of another London performer, the colourful and legendary Screaming Lord Sutch, whose band was called the Savages. (The same Lord Sutch has now become a standard fixture on the English political scene, standing at by-elections all over the country.)

Cyril Davies' new band featured himself as lead vocalist, but he also had a back-up vocalist – another stalwart of the London blues scene,

Long John Baldry. Baldry would sing, which allowed Cyril Davies to play harmonica. Cyril also added four black South African singers as backing vocalists, who went under the name of the Velvettes. The singers had been touring in a musical version of *King Kong* and according to Geoff Bradford they were quite a sight to see.

The lead guitar player in this first line up was a guitarist called Bernie Watson. However, Cyril Davies was not satisfied with what Bernie was playing. Bernie, though, was a fine guitar player. One of the members of the audience that admired Cyril's band was a teenager called Eric Clapton. He remembers:

> *'They were a fantastic band. Bernie Watson was the first guy I ever saw bending notes and the first I ever saw playing a twin-cut-away Gibson semi-acoustic. He always sat down with his back to the audience and never stood up. A very mysterious man.'*

The drummer in that group was Carlo Little, who remembers another side of Cyril's personality:

> *'We started out as a co-operative, but then Cyril got a bit bossy. We complained and he said: "I've got you all covered." He had lined up guys to replace us if we got uppity. We couldn't cope with that sort of atmosphere so one by one we left.'*

One of those who left early on was guitarist Bernie Watson. He then joined up with a new blues musician in town who had just arrived at the invitation of 'The guv'nor' Alexis Korner, who was busily introducing him to the London scene. This new arrival's name was, of course, John Mayall, and Bernie Watson joined John Mayall's new band to which John had given the name the Bluesbreakers. I'm sure you are going to guess what I'm going to say next... of whom more later! Eventually Geoff Bradford got the call from Cyril Davies and was invited to join the R&B Allstars as lead guitarist. Alexis Korner remembers:

'Cyril Davies was definitely aiming to be a working class hero. It was always his intensity that struck you.'

Back we go again to the personalities of Charley Patton, Son House and Robert Johnson – lots of intensity. Geoff Bradford, however, remembers another side of Cyril Davies:

'I remember one day walking down the street with Cyril and complaining as I often did, about my guitar sound. I was always unhappy with it. Just at that moment we were passing a music shop and there in the window was a brand new Fender Telecaster. Cyril walked straight into the shop and bought it for me there and then. So there I was at the next gig on the stage with a brand new Telecaster.'

Geoff Bradford was to become very well known for his Telecaster lead guitar playing and a couple of his younger admirers were Jeff Beck and Jimmy Page – two future guitar heroes of the sixties.

Tragically Cyril Davies contracted pleurisy, after which he started drinking quite heavily to ease the pain. He was advised by his doctor to stop gigging. However, he ignored the advice and eventually he turned yellow and had to walk with a stick. He died on 7 January, 1964 aged thirty-one. The cause of death was given as endocarditis.

So the London R&B scene had lost one of its founding fathers. A tremendous singer, band leader and harmonica player; someone that could reproduce the music of Leadbelly with his twelve-string guitar. His death left a huge gaping hole in the scene. Alexis Korner had moved away from straight R&B into a more jazzy kind of rhythm and blues. But a younger audience had been turned on to both of them. The Rolling Stones had formed and were beginning to get their own gigs.

After Cyril's death, Long John Baldry took over the group and re-named it the Hoochie Coochie Men recruiting his own back-up vocalist, one Rod Stewart who, legend has it, Baldry had discovered singing in a drunken stupor on Twickenham railway station. The Hoochie Coochie Men were named after another famous Muddy Waters track. Archivist Pete Frame remembers seeing Baldry's band at the Grosvenor, Aylesbury:

> *'Geoff Bradford, the first guy on the scene playing a Telecaster as a lead instrument, is exceptional. If he had joined John Mayall when he got that call he would be world famous... fabulous!!!'*

Chapter 9

Lead guitar heroes

Geoff Bradford was the first English blues lead guitar hero. Having re-joined Cyril Davies in the Allstars, Geoff began to get a reputation among the blues audience as a lead guitar player. He was the first person to use the Fender Telecaster as a lead instrument. Geoff told me later:

'I was not aware of gaining any kind of reputation at first as a lead guitar hero. However, you need to remember that up until that time there had not been any lead guitar heroes. The Fender Telecaster had been used as a rhythm instrument and not for lead guitar playing. Another thing is that amplifiers, when I first started playing, were tiny; they looked like old-fashioned radio receivers and I remember on occasions actually playing through the same little amplifier as the bass player. I was always worried about my guitar sound and this was because I was trying to re-produce the sound of T-Bone Walker, Hubert Sumlin and Willie Johnson.'

While playing in Cyril Davies' band Geoff Bradford was kept on a fairly tight rein.

'Cyril was a very strict band leader. He knew exactly what he wanted to hear and he would often come right up to me and sing the part he wanted me to play on guitar, right in my face. He was a perfectionist and he wanted the band to sound exactly right and there was not much opportunity for stretching out on lead guitar. I used to play tight guitar breaks that were closer to the kind of break you might hear from a saxophone or harmonica. After Cyril died and Long John Baldry took over the band, all this began to change. I had much more freedom to stretch out as a lead guitarist in the Baldry band. In my opinion the Baldry band was actually a better group.'

At that time Geoff Bradford got to know Jimmy Page quite well as Jimmy was having a successful time playing session guitar for various pop acts. Jimmy admired Geoff as a player. Jimmy Page represented a new generation of guitarists and was one of a famous group of English lead guitar players who were to transform over a period of five years the whole concept of the guitarist within a band.

Jimmy Page was born 9 January, 1944. Jeff Beck was born on 24 June, 1944, Eric Clapton was born on 30 March, 1945 and Peter Green was born on 29 October, 1946. Therefore in 1965, Peter Green was nineteen, Eric Clapton was twenty and Jimmy Page and Jeff Beck were both twenty-one years old. Geoff Bradford, however, who was born on 13 January, 1934 in Highbury, London was already thirty-one years old; John Mayall was thirty-two and Alexis Korner was thirty-seven.

This younger generation of guitarists grew up listening to a different kind of American musician. Although they all listened to many of the American players we have already discussed, it was Eric Clapton and Peter Green's interest in the likes of Otis Rush, B.B. King, Freddie King, Buddy Guy and Matt Murphy that were to cause a big change in the profile of the guitar player in an English blues band.

By the time 1965 had come round, Geoff Bradford had left Long John Baldry's Hoochie Coochie Men and was, as you will remember, suffering from a nervous breakdown. It was in the same year that Eric Clapton left the Yardbirds and joined John Mayall's Bluesbreakers and it is to Eric Clapton's story that we must now turn.

Chapter 10

Eric Clapton

Eric Clapton was born in Ripley, Surrey. His natural father's name was Edward Walter Fryer. Edward Fryer was a Canadian serving in the 14th Canadian Hussars and had arrived in England in 1942. He is remembered by an Army colleague Neal Hunter as being 'essentially uncomplicated but a sensitive guy off to himself most of the time'. He also is remembered for playing the piano.

In 1944, Fryer met and got to know a local teenager named Patricia Clapton who was born 7 January, 1929. Pat's father, an articled clerk whose name was Reginald, died in 1933 and her mother, Rose, eventually became re-married to a man named Jack Clapp, who was a plasterer and bricklayer. The family settled at No. 1 The Green, Ripley, Surrey. Ripley was a typical English village and 1 The Green was a four-bedroomed redbrick dwelling which had a tiny garden and an outside lavatory.

Pat Clapton was a very good looking young lady and had met Edward Fryer at a local dance. As a result of their liaison she became pregnant at the age of fifteen. Jack and Rose Clapp were very shocked when they heard the news and the pregnancy was the talk of the village. In those times teenage pregnancy was socially stigmatised and there was much cruel gossip in the village. Patricia Clapton gave birth to her baby early on 30 March, 1945. The baby was delivered at the family's home by Rose and the local midwife. The baby was a boy and was christened Eric Patrick Clapton. (The name Clapton is derived from the old English 'Clop', denoting a bulky or sturdy character.)

Patricia Clapton kept the baby for two years, but she eventually left Ripley and Eric Clapton was raised by his grandparents. Although Jack and Rose never actually legally adopted Eric, they were his guardians until 1963.

From the start Eric had a reputation for being 'different'. He was quiet, very moody, but extremely polite. He had a love of animals and had a pet Labrador as well as snails. He got to know a pony that grazed from time to time on Ripley Green. He began to develop a talent for drawing, but all of his pictures were of inanimate objects – there were no people in them.

Having gone through his first school he ended up at St Bedes Secondary Modern. He is remembered as being a 'distant kid'; he was a loner and did not take part in any sport except for the occasional boxing match, which was staged in Guy Pullen's – one of Clapton's few friends – back garden.

An event in 1956 was to change Clapton's life. His mother visited Clapton. She had been living in Canada and accompanying her on her visit was her six year old son. The effect on Eric Clapton was profound. He became moody and nasty, and stopped trying at school. He had to go through the whole pretence that his mother was in fact his sister while she was visiting, presumably was to protect her six year old son.

Whatever the reason for this visit it changed Eric Clapton's personality. Eventually, Clapton ended up at Hollyfields School and by the time he was thirteen he had turned into a belligerent adolescent, with narrow eyes and a downturned mouth. At school he was known by his nickname 'Loonie'. Eric was good at art and eventually managed to achieve a place for himself at Kingston Art College. During this period he had come across the music of Little Richard and Buddy Holly, as well as that of Jerry Lee Lewis, who were some of the first rock 'n' rollers to cross the Atlantic. He also began to hear the music of Chuck Berry.

On BBC radio at that time there was a children's programme called *Uncle Mac's Hour*. Strangely enough Uncle Mac would occasionally play a Sonny Terry harmonica record or a Memphis Slim boogie piece. It was through rock 'n' roll that Eric Clapton began to go deeper into American music and discover the blues.Eric Clapton remembers:

'I felt through most of my youth that my back was against the wall and that the only way to survive was with dignity, pride and courage. I heard that in certain forms of music and I heard it most of all in the blues, because it was always an individual. It was one man and his guitar versus the world. It wasn't a company, or a band or a group. When it came down to it, it was one guy who was completely alone and had no options, no alternatives other than just to sing and play to ease his pains. And that echoes what I felt.'

With the kind of background that Eric Clapton had it's easy to see why he would associate himself with the blues. Throughout all his formative years he had a feeling of being different and on his own. Significantly, this put him in exactly the right state of mind to be able to appreciate the music of Robert Johnson, for Robert Johnson's voice carries such a feeling of displacement and embitterment it might have been an exact manifestation of Eric's state of mind.

Clapton set out to listen to as much blues as he possibly could and in 1958, Eric persuaded Rose and Jack to buy him his first acoustic guitar. By the end of that year, Eric and his guitar were inseparable. Eric practised and practised and rapidly began to gain technical facility on the instrument.

After starting at Kingston Art College, Eric began roaming further afield and armed with a newly acquired Green Line bus pass he began to discover Twickenham, Richmond and then London. Clapton, like Geoff Bradford before him, discovered Dobells music shop and it was through this shop and Potters Music Shop in Richmond, that he was able to hear more and more American blues performers. Eric Clapton began to play guitar sitting on Richmond Green and playing the music of country blues guitar stars such as Big Bill Broonzy, Brownie McGhee and Muddie Waters.

In 1962, once again he persuaded his grandparents to invest in another guitar. This time it was an electric guitar. The guitar was a Kay Red Devil, which was a cheap imitation of a Gibson ES 335. Eric had acquired for himself a reel-to-reel tape recorder and would spend hours trying to perfect his guitar style. He started to attend the Marquee and the Ealing Club. Eventually he found the courage to get up on stage and sing. However, he did so without a guitar and Dick Heckstall-Smith, who was at that time a member of Alexis Korner's Blues Incorporated, remembers it like this...

'...pale sulky kid who came on stage, with no guitar, sung two songs and fled. I wasn't exactly knocked out.'

At this time Eric Clapton supported himself through a number of jobs on building sites and at one time as a relief postman. Eventually, Clapton was to meet another guitarist called Tom McGuinness. They formed a group together called the Roosters, which lasted for about six months. The pianist in the group, who was to become one of Eric Clapton's closest friends, was a man named Ben Palmer.

One quality that Ben Palmer remembers about Eric Clapton was that he 'loved to take guitar solos'. This was most unusual as you needed tremendous confidence to actually put your neck on the block this way. This quality of Eric Clapton's was in direct contrast to his personality off stage, which was that of a shy brooding loner. Another thing Palmer remembers about Clapton was that he had...

'...a marked sense of timing. He seemed to know exactly when,

*and when not to, cut loose. There was something uncanny
about it.'*

One of the first regular gigs for the newly formed Rolling Stones was
at a club in Richmond, held in the back room of a pub opposite
Richmond station called the Station Hotel. Eventually the Rolling
Stones' following became too large for the club and the Stones moved
on. They were replaced by new local group called the Yardbirds who
had got their name from the jazz horn player Charlie 'Yardbird' Parker.

This group had as members Tony Topham, Jim McCarty, Chris Dreja
and Keith Relf with a Twickenham local, Paul Samwell-Smith, who
originally played guitar. Paul Samwell-Smith rapidly switched to the
bass guitar and Tony Topham fulfilled the lead guitar role. However, he
didn't last long as he was under pressure from his parents to return to
Art School, which left the band without a guitarist. However, Keith Relf
knew of another guitar player who regularly used to play at the Crown
in Kingston – and thus Eric Clapton was approached. Apparently he
was seen as some kind of James Dean figure who would be able to
'pull' the women.

Rose and Jack Clapp had to co-sign the contract as Eric's guardians
in November 1963... and Eric Clapton was in the Yardbirds. Chris Dreja
began to play rhythm guitar allowing Eric to take the lead guitar role.

At that time Chris Dreja and Jim McCarty remember Eric as a
comedian who would change his appearance and his hairstyle all the
time. Clapton was very defensive and had extreme mood swings. He
could be vicious and would send up other members of the band.

The Yardbirds first began recording on the 1 November, 1963 and
they recorded a demo of Jimmy Read's 'Baby What's Wrong' and John
Lee Hooker's 'Boom Boom', finishing the session with Billie Boy
Arnold's 'Honey In Your Hips'. Eventually the Yardbirds' manager,
Giorgio Gomelsky, signed the group to EMI Records and the band
released their debut single 'I Wish You Would' in early 1964.

Clapton's playing on the single's B side, 'A Certain Girl', already
displayed his potential and by this time he was using a Fender

Telecaster. A point worth noting is that according to Jim McCarty, Eric Clapton took to studio recording 'like a bird to the air'. According to Chris Dreja there was a certain 'sweetness' about Eric Clapton's guitar playing, which he attributes to 'pure God-given talent, as anyone could tell'. As a guitar player Eric was already beginning to become a bit of a star.

On 7 and 8 December, 1963 the Yardbirds appeared on stage at the Station Hotel in Richmond with Sonny Boy Williamson (Rice Miller). You will remember from earlier in the book that Sonny Boy had actually known Robert Johnson and was present on the night he died, so by coincidence and fate Eric Clapton had ended up meeting and playing with someone who had actually known his great hero. Sonny Boy Williamson was at that time living in England because he had received such acclaim there and was exploiting the new young white English blues audience.

Sonny Boy Williamson did not have a very attractive personality. He was often drunk and didn't think much of the indigenous white blues performers. Geoff Bradford also played with Sonny Boy Williamson and remembers him as 'arrogant' and 'dismissive'. Williamson's comments on the Yardbirds were:

'These boys want to play the blues very badly and that's how they played the blues... very badly.'

Sonny Boy Williamson certainly looked bizarre at the time, having decided to wear an English bowler hat and dress suit on the stage. Apparently, Eric Clapton was somewhat more forgiving of Sonny Boy Williamson's behaviour than was Geoff Bradford, excusing him in the light of the fact that he had 'suffered'.

From early on Eric Clapton did not get on with Paul Samwell-Smith – apparently not thinking much of his bass playing abilities. Throughout his long career Eric has always had the reputation of finding something wrong with his current musical line up. He's just that kind of person.

On 13 March, 1964 the Yardbirds were recorded live during a residency that they were playing at the London Marquee club. (This you will remember was the club that Alexis Korner and Cyril Davies had played at in their pioneering Thursday night rhythm and blues sessions.) An album was released of these recordings called *Five Live Yardbirds*. It appeared in December 1964, but didn't sell that well. The publicist for the Yardbirds at that time was a man named Hamish Grimes, who was trying to hype the Yardbirds as being credible rivals to the Rolling Stones, putting them forward, in fact, as another Rolling Stones. However, the *London Times* retorted: 'The Rolling Stones wrote 'Satisfaction''.

This hype was really ridiculous as the Yardbirds were not to come anywhere near the popularity and success of the Rolling Stones. This little battle of the bands reminds me of the battle between T-Bone Walker and Muddy Waters on the Chicago blues scene.

Anyway, the real star of *Five Live Yardbirds* is undoubtedly Eric Clapton. His guitar solo on 'Too Much Monkey Business' displayed an aggression which was totally new and his playing in general was a revelation. According to critic Don Short, it was then that some people *did* compare the Yardbirds to the Stones because of Eric Clapton.

A split was beginning to emerge between Eric Clapton and Gomelsky's efforts to create a pop band. Eric Clapton didn't want to have anything to do with pop music at the time. He saw himself as being a blues player. On stage Eric would stand still, sometimes playing with his back to the audience which you will remember Bernie Watson used to do. This was still very unusual, but Eric was probably doing it because he could get certain feedback sounds out of his amplifier.

Eric Clapton was concentrating more and more on his guitar playing and less and less on stardom. The Yardbirds were going in the opposite direction. Gomelsky was to give Eric his famous nickname of 'Slow hands' as a kind of ironic comment on Eric's guitar prowess. Eric Clapton was gaining a following in his own right and it was during this time that the concept of lead guitar hero, which had been started off by Geoff Bradford, really began to take off.

It is important to realise though, that the audience for Eric Clapton and the Yardbirds was of a different generation to the one that had been watching Alexis Korner and Cyril Davies. This younger audience was not made up of blues or jazz enthusiasts. By this time the Beatles and the Rolling Stones had happened and the younger audience was more typical of those bands' following than they were of the older blues jazz generation. Therefore, as has previously been pointed out, for them Clapton's playing was an entirely new and very exciting experience. They didn't know much of the blues, they just knew that Clapton was exciting.

In the first weeks of 1965, while the Yardbirds were playing in Richmond, Chris Drejar met Jeff Beck, a twenty year old guitarist who had been playing in an interval band at Eel Pie Island in Twickenham, which had been another stronghold of the Cyril Davies and Long John Baldry blues bands. Geoff Bradford remembers Jeff Beck at that time as being already a very promising blues guitarist. Drejar apparently had heard of Jeff Beck as being a 'wayward genius' and since Eric Clapton was beginning to show his displeasure with the Yardbirds, targeted Jeff Beck as a potential replacement.

Matters finally came to a head when at a recording session at IBC Studios, Manager Gomelsky announce that the group were to record a pop song written by songwriter Graham Gouldman called 'For Your Love'. That was it for Eric Clapton and he decided to leave. He had had enough and he returned to Ripley.

However, when it was released in March 1965, the B side of the single featured an instrumental composition by Eric Clapton called 'Got To Hurry'. In stark contrast to the A side this instrumental was reminiscent of the Chicago blues of Otis Rush, Freddie King and Buddy Guy. This track was to prove very important to Clapton's future because it impressed John Mayall who had already seen Eric Clapton in the Yardbirds and wasn't at that time, that impressed with him. That changed with the release of 'Got To Hurry'.

Chapter 11

Peter Green

Although only one year younger than Eric Clapton, Peter Green was an entirely different person to him. Peter came from a tough East End of London background. However, he grew up in a happy, stable family with two brothers – Len the elder and Michael who was born in August 1940 – and a sister Linda, who was born in 1942.

Peter was born at 27 Bullen House, off the Mile End Road, on 29 October, 1946. He was born with the surname Greenbaum, and his family were typically East End Jewish. Because Peter's father had been in Bethnall Green for a long time and had lived at the rough end around Brady Street and Whitechapel, he had experienced the discrimination that was enacted against Jewish people before and after the war.

Having heard some kids shouting out abuse, Peter's brother Michael remembers that his father decided to change the family name to Green by deed-poll. Peter seems to have grown up a happy child. However, years later one of Peter's girlfriends, named Sandra, remembers that he apparently burst into tears on one occasion. He sobbed and talked about how painful it was for a little boy being Jewish. He said he had been teased and taunted and, to her, the scars were obviously still there. Peter's brother Michael, remembers one instance that seemed to show an early sensitivity in Peter. He had taken Peter, then a seven year old, to see the film *Bambi*, and they had found the film very moving. Later at home, Michael started to hum the tune from the film and Peter burst into tears. He burst into tears, according to Michael, because he loved animals.

In the late 1940s, Peter's father Jo, changed his job from that of a tailor to working in the post office, at first working as a postman in Bethnall Green. However, Peter's father had health problems and in 1956 the family moved out of the East End into a larger flat in Linton Avenue, Putney.

The move made Peter Green very happy. Putney, as it turns out, is a bus ride away from Richmond in Surrey, and a world away from the East End of London.

Peter, who like Eric Clapton had a liking for pets, ended up at Elliot Comprehensive School, which was on Putney Hill. I used to play basketball against Elliot School and I remember it very well. It was a brand new building and incredibly well equipped. At Elliot, Peter Green did well and was obviously very bright.

Also Like Eric Clapton, Peter was not that good at sport and the school had every kind of sports facilities. It was a very large school with 1,500 children. At school Peter was a quiet boy, although according to Ed Spevock, he was well liked.

Peter was to take up the guitar, but he told me later in an interview that I did with him when he lived round the corner from me in Richmond, that he hadn't taken to the guitar very easily and found it difficult initially to learn chords. However, while at school Peter had joined a school band with his brother Michael. Peter Anderton, another one of Peter's school friends, became the drummer in the group. He remembers:

'We rehearsed at a flat in Walham Grove, Fulham and at Peter's parents' flat in Putney.'

Peter was taking the lead guitar role and even then was a talented guitarist. Peter Anderson also remembers Peter as...

'...a very popular guy, very laid back and always courteous.'

Despite the fact that Peter was slim and of only average height, he was quite a tough kid. Ed Spevock remembers that...

'...he knew how to handle himself.'

Peter Green remembers that on several occasions he used to have boxing matches with other kids at the school. He said:

'I guess I had about half a dozen fights and won them all.'

Although Peter Green was in one of the high groups at school he actually left without any formal qualifications. He was keen to get out into the wide world and earn some money. He was encouraged by his brother, Len, to try trainee butchering. Peter got a job at a butchers shop called David Gregg's in Fulham High Street. He was very good at this job and stayed there for two years. During this time he began to develop greatly as a musician. However, he told me:

'In the end I didn't serve an apprenticeship. I just went as another member of the shop. I wasn't good at it at all; I couldn't master it. There was a feeling you had when you had mastered it, but I never got anything.'

However, by the end of the year Peter could break down a side of beef into cuts and the manager told him:

'You're a good butcher, you have learnt really well.'

It was typical of Peter at the time I interviewed him early in the 1980s to be very self-effacing about any of his achievements. Peter started to play bass guitar. He had been attracted to the bass because he loved the look of it and his brother Michael lent him the deposit for a bass called a Star. He remembers:

'It cost me £40 and it was really a beautiful thing.'

Peter started out playing the music of the Beatles and the Hollies, and he managed to get into a band called the Tridents, eventually ending up in the spring of 1965 after playing in a number of other local bands in a group called the Muskrats. It was during this time with the Muskrats – approximately six months or so – that Peter began to hear old 78s by people like Muddy Waters. One track that he heard was 'Honey Bee', which he talked about as 'very spare and together' (which would have been quite a nice way of describing Peter's later guitar sound).

Also during this time, Peter saw both the Yardbirds and the Rolling Stones playing at Richmond's Crawdaddy club. He admired Bill Wyman of the Rolling Stones because of the way he would stand with a serious pose at the back of the band, playing the bass – obviously more pre-occupied with the music than with being a showman.

However, it was seeing Eric Clapton playing in the Yardbirds that was to change Peter's life. He later told me that part of the reason he switched from bass to guitar was because of his desire to make it as a professional musician, and by this time the role of lead guitarist had taken on something of a more charismatic profile than playing bass.

Peter was supported by his father and mother in his quest to become a musician and in that sense he was lucky, for most parents of the time disapproved of the new music. In his hunt to get work as a guitarist, Peter would scan the Musicians Wanted page of *Melody Maker* and also hang around the offices of the Gunnell Brothers agency, hoping that something might turn up. In February 1966, it did.

Robert Johnson

'Blind' Willie McTell

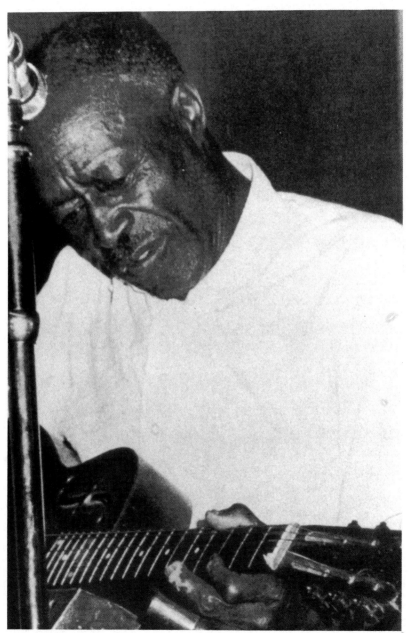

Sonny House

Muddy Waters at the Newport jazz festival in 1960

Blind Blake

Alexis Korner

Mick Taylor and Keef Hartley, 1967

Eric Clapton at the Windsor festival in 1967

Mayall, in the dressing room after playing at the Marquee in August 1968

Led Zeppelin in 1968 (clockwise Jimmy Page, John Bonham, John Paul Jones and Robert Plant)

Mayall on stage in 1968

Peter Green with Fleetwood Mac, May 1969 (clockwise, Danny Kirwan, Mick Fleetwood, Peter Green, John McVie and Jeremy Spencer)

Free in 1969 (clockwise, Simon Kirke, Andy Fraser, Paul Kossoff, and Paul Rodgers)

Mayall at the Town & Country Club, 1992

Rick and Jonnie Gunnell owned the Flamingo club in Wardour Street, an all-night venue that attracted American GIs. The Gunnells also owned the Bag O' Nails and the Ram Jam club in Brixton. They had recently put together a new band called Peter B's Looners describing them as 'masters of cool blue pop'. They had been modelled on the Stax/Atlantic soul band of Booker T. & the MGs, who had a hit with an instrumental called 'Green Onions'. At the start of 1966, Peter B's Looners were looking for a new guitar player. Apparently Peter Green put himself forward for this band. The band was run by Peter Bardens. When he saw Green the first thing he said to him was:

'So you wanna be our new guitarist do you? Well, those sideburns will have to come off right away.'

Apparently Peter was speechless, but later publicity shots showed that the sideburns had remained. Other members of the band at that time included Dave Ambrose on bass, and a long lanky drummer called Mick Fleetwood. Fleetwood and Ambrose critically adjudged this new guitar player as 'not being up to much'. However, Peter Bardens had a different view of Peter Green's talents, saying:

'You're both wrong; this guy's got a great talent, he's going to be great.'

Bardens described Peter's playing as follows.

'Pete played that very simplified incisive clean style perfectly. In a short space of time he changed from hacking out a few clichés to developing a style and playing with a lot of power, becoming a real contender. He had a raw talent and because we played so much in those days – too much if anything – he really honed it.'

The band used to play right through the weekends at the Marquee, the Ram Jam and the Flamingo clubs, and recorded one single before changing its name to Shotgun Express. This single was Peter Green's first experience of a recording studio. It was called 'If You Wanna Be Happy' and the B side was 'Jodrell Blues'.

According to Peter Bardens, Peter Green, just like Eric Clapton, had taken to the studio situation without any problems at all. Eventually, Rod Stewart was to join the band along with Beryl Marsden, and Shotgun Express became a vocal group.

In the summer of 1966, Peter Green had moved into a flat in Bayswater's Porchester Road. Living in the same block was John Mayall.

Chapter 12

Learning to play guitar in the early sixties

At this point I feel it would be useful to look at some aspects of learning to the play the guitar at this period of time. In the early sixties there were hardly any instruction books available. Geoff Bradford remembers getting hold of a copy of a basic guitar instruction tutor published by Mel Blay. There was also a very thin instruction book called *Play In A Day*, which had been written by an older generation London session guitarist called Bert Weedon, who had had a number of instrumental hits in the fifties. Other than that though, there wasn't much, and what there was tended to concentrate on folk music. Therefore, most of what could be learned had to come from listening to the records of the great blues guitarists that were coming on to the market.

Bradford, Green and Clapton all used a similar method of playing and replaying records and learning by heart the musical riffs played by the guitar players. A riff is a short musical phrase and if you strung enough of these together, you could create a whole guitar solo. Undoubtedly the master of this technique was Eric Clapton. However, as time went by and more and more technical facility was developed, the guitarist would begin to find his way around the fretboard.

For Bradford, Eric Clapton and Peter Green, the most important fact was that they wanted the guitar and the amp to sound right. Interestingly enough, what sounded right to one guitarist would definitely not sound right to another, so this is where you get an element of personal choice beginning to enter the situation. This accounts for the very different guitar sounds of Peter Green, Eric Clapton and Geoff Bradford.

The process of trying to find the right sound was to carry on throughout the sixties with each new star guitar player becoming known for his own particular sound. Indeed, it was by virtue of the fact that a guitarist had his own distinctive sound and style that first drew the attention of the public. If you think of the playing of Jimmy Page, Paul Kossoff (of the rock band Free) and of course Jimi Hendrix, you will see my point. They all had their own distinct sound.

Mention should be made in this chapter about a parallel musical movement that was going on at the same time as the development of the British blues scene. A whole set of acoustic guitarists began to emerge dedicated to playing acoustic blues. The earliest of these was Davy Graham, who you will remember was a regular at the Round House along with Geoff Bradford in the early days; and Geoff Bradford himself was an accomplished acoustic blues guitarist at that time. Shortly after this, Wizz Jones and Cliff Aungier were also to make their presence felt on the London scene.

Round about the same time, the finest twelve-string guitarist that Europe has ever produced, John Joyce, was also beginning to play in public. It was John Joyce who eventually became one of my mentors and was responsible for introducing me to Geoff Bradford and Brian Knight in the early seventies. John Joyce is also a very well-known guitar repairer and shared with Alexis Korner a generosity of spirit. He has become both an educator and a friend.

The early folk scene in London was to attract a Scottish guitarist called Bert Jansch, who was to be a major influence on the acoustic guitar development of Jimmy Page who would eventually, as we shall see, blend elements of British acoustic guitar music and traditional folk themes with blues and rock 'n' roll in the music of one of the biggest rock bands of all time, Led Zeppelin.

Chapter 13

John Mayall's Bluesbreakers

John Mayall was born in Macclesfield, Cheshire on 29 November, 1933. During his teenage years he had learnt the guitar and the piano, and his father was a jazz enthusiast with a large collection of jazz records. His father played in dance bands in his spare time, but was never able to make a living at it.

Mayall, like Eric Clapton, was talented at art and when he was thirteen years old, went to a Junior Art School in Manchester and completed a two-year course. When he left school he managed to find a local job doing window display work at a department store. He worked his way up in to the drawing office of the same store. The work involved putting on exhibitions and other display work at the store, such as Christmas decorations.

John worked at the store for two years before being conscripted into the Army to do his national service. He spent some time in Korea and on his return went to the Regional College of Art in Manchester, doing a four year course from 1955–1959. When he left, he got a job in an art studio, which was attached to an advertising agency.

He had already begun to collect blues records and while he was at college, he formed and led his first band, called the Powerhouse Four. They had a drummer called Peter Ward who John would work with again in a later version of the Bluesbreakers.

John seemed to have been a bit of an eccentric in those days – a reputation that was to increase when he took up residence in a tree-house that he had built for himself in Acre Lane, Cheadle Hulme, Cheshire. Apparently, this tree house had been equipped by John with running water, a bed, a stove and even a gramophone, carpets and wallpaper. As reported in the *Manchester Evening News* at the time:

> *'Here as he sways thirty feet above the ground, jazzman [now that's a term worth remembering for the future] John practises on his guitar and listens to his favourite music.'*

John would attend the local clubs and you will remember it was in 1961 that he saw Alexis Korner and Cyril Davies play at Manchester's Twisted Wheel. John decided to form his own band, a new band called the Blues Syndicate. Hughie Flint was its drummer and he remembers:

> *'I first ran into John Mayall in Manchester around 1957 or '58. I was in a crowd of friends who dragged me up to a youth centre in Wythenshawe where John was a so-called teacher. It was one of those twice a week things where he was paid by the council to get musical events organised and to teach kids to play instruments. It was a real hotch-potch of jazz, blues and skiffle. We used to go up there and jam. John played marvellous barrelhouse piano and a bit of harmonica and guitar. We became very good friends and I would go to his house every weekend. He had shelves and shelves of tapes and hundreds of records. It was just incredible.'*

At the beginning of 1963, John Mayall, now twenty-nine years old, took up Alexis Korner's invitation and went to London to make his name.

Between January and March 1963, John Mayall tried to form a band. He rehearsed with various different players including folk guitarist Davy Graham who you will remember had been a regular at the Round House club along with Geoff Bradford. However, none of these rehearsals worked out. It was then that John Mayall was to find bass player John McVie.

From 1963 onwards, the London R&B scene really began to take off with a new generation as its audience. The Rolling Stones, Manfred Mann and the Yardbirds were all beginning to make their way. More and more blues recordings by the American greats were becoming available in this country.

John Mayall signed a management agency deal with Rick Gunnell and started to play the club circuit. His main base of operations was at Gunnell's Flamingo Club, which became a mecca for the second wave of R&B. Having got to London and started trying to put his band together, Mayall decided to call his new group the Bluesbreakers. This name was a very good choice as it seemed to convey to anyone coming across it for the first time exactly what the band was about. It was a name that carried its own objective, that of breaking the blues to a wider audience. 'Breaking a record' was a sixties term referring to popularising that record with the general public – that is, breaking it through to a new audience. So therefore Mayall was trying to 'break the blues'.

John McVie, up until that time, had been in a Shadows-style group. The Shadows were an instrumental guitar group and one of their most famous hits was 'Apache'. On connecting with John Mayall, McVie was given a stack of records and told to go and listen to them so that he could find out how the blues were played. McVie remembers:

'When we started to play, John Mayall said: "OK, let's try a twelve-bar in C", and I had to ask him what he meant. So he told me, "Just follow my chords."'

Over the next twelve months, John McVie was to learn how to play bass in a blues band.

It was at this time that John Mayall, as a band leader, instigated an open-door policy which was very similar to the one that had been employed by Cyril Davies and Alexis Korner in Blues Incorporated. We need to remember that the scene was very small and that musicians would come and go from bands on a regular basis. So therefore, initially it was Alexis Korner that was the star, or Cyril Davies or John Mayall. Artists were billed by name followed by their band name – that is, Cliff Richard and the Shadows, or Cyril Davies and the Allstars. Geoff Bradford remembers this time very well and later he told me:

> *'Working with Cyril Davies was very much like having a day job. It was what you did; you got your wages, it was your job. You were there to back Cyril and not necessarily there to express any of your own musical ideas. In Cyril Davies' case if you got out of line, you would soon be called up short and if Cyril didn't like what you were doing, you were out.'*

Musicians at that time had no security at all. They were very much part of the main man's band and subject to his whim. If you were a main man like John Mayall, the most important thing was to get your name round the clubs so that you got a reputation for playing a certain kind of music.

New bands were forming all the time and the situation gets very complicated in the early sixties as more and more young people formed groups both to imitate the newly popular Liverpool pop bands such as the Beatles, Gerry and the Pacemakers and so on, and also to try to play rhythm and blues and rock 'n' roll.

John Mayall's open-door policy became something of a legend. You were in the band when Mayall decided he needed you and you were out again just as quickly when he had had enough of you. But gradually a change began to take place in the longevity of these groups caused by the fact that instrumentalists such as lead guitar players and keyboard players began to get reputations in their own right, and if you had one of these players in your band they were very difficult to replace.

During the period that we are interested in, which runs roughly from 1963 through to the late sixties, John Mayall had an almost magical touch when it came to finding the right musicians for the Bluesbreakers. Between July 1963 and April 1964, the Bluesbreakers finally settled down into a permanent line up. This was John Mayall on keyboards, vocals and harmonica, John McVie on the bass, Bernie Watson on guitar, who had joined having played with Cyril Davies (you will remember that Bernie Watson was replaced by Geoff Bradford in Cyril Davies' band after Cyril had decided that Bernie Watson's playing was not quite right for his sound) and Peter Ward on drums, who had played in Mayall's college band, the Powerhouse Four.

Ward was subsequently replaced by Martin Hart on drums. Peter Ward had left because he didn't want to go on the road full time, and Martin Hart was a replacement until Hughie Flint could join Mayall from Manchester. Mayall had managed to get a day job for himself as a draughtsman. However, having signed the management agency deal with Rick Gunnell, he was able to turn fully professional in the early part of 1964.

It was at that time – April 1964 – that Hughie Flint was able to join the band. They were doing about five gigs a week, but things were about to change as Bernie Watson (who was to go on to become a respected classical guitarist in later life) left the group. He was replaced by Roger Dean – a strange choice because his music was rooted in the guitar style of Chet Atkins, who was much more known for his country guitar styles rather than blues. During the changeover from Watson to Dean, Mayall had tried out a lot of other players, but no one seemed to quite fit the bill.

When Roger Dean eventually joined, John Mayall spent a lot of time trying to explain to him exactly what he wanted him to play and how he wanted him to sound. This line-up was to record a single called 'Crocodile Walk'/'Blues City Shakedown', which came out in early 1965. Previously, the group with Bernie Watson in it had recorded a single called 'Crawling Up A Hill'/'Mr James', which came out in April 1964.

Nothing much happened popularity-wise regarding these first

105

releases. However, John Mayall was already beginning to write his own blues songs, and undoubtedly an influence was the music of the Chicago blues man J.B. Lenoir, as has already been noted. Song-writing was a big departure from what Alexis Korner and Cyril Davies had been doing, as they were mostly content to recycle the music of the American greats and had little interest in writing their own songs.

John Mayall's Bluesbreakers recorded their first blues album, *John Mayall Plays John Mayall*, which was released in March 1965. The album was recorded live at a club called Klooks Kleek in West Hampstead. This club was right next door to Decca's recording studio and the recording was done by simply trailing some microphone cables from the studio into the club.

The album featured two original compositions by John Mayall plus two R&B favourites, 'Night Train' and 'Lucille'. In the future Mayall would describe this album as 'terrible'.

Archivist Pete Frame remembers seeing this John Mayall line-up at the Dunstable Civic Centre in early 1964. He remembers them this way:

'Most impressive. Mayall had a rack of harmonicas hanging around his neck and jumped around at this big old battered organ. John McVie stood at the back serious and practically motionless throughout. Hughie Flint looked like a modern jazzer/erudite beatnik. Roger Dean wore a very neat suit and tie and played an orange Gretsch guitar, and was seated.'

Years and years later, when I was compère at the Cambridge Folk Festival in 1993, John Mayall was on the bill and I was able to watch his performance from the side of the stage. I had also been giving a bottleneck and slide guitar seminar at the festival. John Mayall's act was exactly the same as the early descriptions given by people such as Pete Frame. A most animated performance.

John Mayall was never really happy with Roger Dean's playing and eventually Mayall was to read that Eric Clapton had become unhappy with the Yardbirds and had decided to leave. On one fateful occasion Mayall assembled John McVie and Hughie Flint around the juke-box in

Nottingham and made them listen to the B side of the Yardbirds current single called 'For Your Love'. This was, as you will remember, the instrumental 'Got To Hurry', which featured Eric Clapton playing outright Chicago blues lead guitar much in the style of Freddie King/Buddy Guy/Otis Rush. It's interesting to observe that now this has been re-issued on CD you can hear Clapton's amp buzzing at the beginning of the track. He obviously had it turned up as loud as it would go as this was the only way he was to get the sustain from the guitar and the amp that he required.

This was a new sound as far as the London blues scene was concerned, because guitarists like Bernie Watson, Geoff Bradford and Roger Dean had all played with a clean sound. It is also interesting to recall a comment made by Jeff Beck regarding his early interest in blues guitar, which points out the difference between the guitar sound that Clapton was trying to get and that of the American guitar players. Jeff Beck tells it like this:

'My interest in blues started when the Chicago blues albums began to reach England. I grabbed them. Muddy Waters, Buddy Guy, I thought they were great. There's a special way the guitars sound, sort of tinny and rough; that's a Chicago sound, it's like nothing else.'

It's clear that if you listen to this Chicago sound and then listen to what Eric Clapton was playing on 'Got To Hurry' you can see that Eric may have been playing some of the riffs of the great black guitarists, but he already had his own sound which had much more sustain and which somehow had a thicker texture.

Once Eric Clapton had left the Yardbirds, John Mayall set about trying to find him. He had in fact gone to stay with his friend Ben Palmer in Oxford. Eventually, Mayall tracked him down and telephoned Eric to invite him to join the Bluesbreakers. Roger Dean was then given his marching orders. These are John Mayall's comments on the hiring and firing of musicians:

'There seems to be a nasty stigma attached to the phrase "being fired". It implies a loss of grace or something, that the person being fired is inadequate or even incompetent. But in music it's different; there's usually a reason for it and I don't think it's ever been because the guys couldn't handle their instruments, which is the only area they should feel disgrace about really. It's always been a question of my having played with a particular set of musicians for so long that I need a change. I usually know what I want to do next.'

John Mayall, who had only signed a short-term record contract with Decca, had found that because his records were not selling sufficiently Decca had decided to let him go. This was ironic since with Eric Clapton newly joining the band, the Bluesbreakers were about to take off in a very big way. What had happened was that Eric, who was already seen as a bit of a guitar hero, was to bring his own sizeable following as an instrumentalist to John Mayall gigs.

Eric Clapton, with his almost religious attachment to the blues, found in the rhythm section of the existing Bluesbreakers the vehicle he needed to take him to stardom. People have often commented that Clapton, even at this time, was a shy, self-effacing individual who had no interest in becoming a star. However, this picture of Eric Clapton, I find to be naive. By the time Clapton had left the Yardbirds he had already shown that in his dress, in his guitar playing and in his relationships with other people, they had a good idea what he did want and what he didn't want in his life. He was already on his own road.

Of the time that Eric Clapton joined the Bluesbreakers, John Mayall remembers:

'At the end of our first year the rhythm section of the Bluesbreakers had really solidified. But I had heard only one guitarist in England who could really play the blues, and that was Eric Clapton. At the end of his tenure with the Yardbirds I had heard the B side of their hit single 'For Your Love'; it was an

*instrumental thing called 'Got To Hurry', which was almost
totally in the Freddie King pocket. Freddie was one of my true
idols at the time and Eric was playing in his style. All I can tell
you is what his playing did to me. I didn't analyse it, I just
know it gave me the chills. There was something there that cut
right through me. To have such mastery and feel at that age is
pretty remarkable; it's scary actually. Probably six months
prior I had heard Eric live with the Yardbirds and he wasn't
that impressive, but his improvements were very quick indeed.
It's as if he did all his rough work with the Roosters, made great
strides with the Yardbirds for about a year and then joined the
Bluesbreakers. Once he was in the right environment he
accelerated even more.'*

It was at this time that Eric Clapton changed from playing with a
Telecaster guitar and purchased a Gibson Les Paul guitar. The Les Paul
had been designed by jazz guitarist Les Paul as an instrument that you
could play near to an amplifier without the guitar feeding back. This
requires some explanation...

Up until that time electric guitars had been of the semi-acoustic
variety. This meant that the guitar, although not having the same
characteristics as a fully blown acoustic guitar, did retain a hollow body,
which contributed to the sound of the instrument.

The problem was that if you got too close to your amplifier, the air
inside the hollow body would start to vibrate. This vibration would
then be transferred back into the amplifier and you would get
feedback, a kind of howling sound (later used to great effect by Pete
Townsend, Jeff Beck and Jimi Hendrix).

Les Paul used a solid plank of wood for his guitar; therefore the
body of the guitar was completely solid, thus reducing feedback.
However, to achieve the kind of tone he wanted he used two
humbucker pickups. These pickups gave a rich, warm bassy sound to
the guitar. They were very responsive and subtle when compared with
the sound created by the Fender Telecaster (which Geoff Bradford had

first used and had been adopted by Eric Clapton), which used a single coil pickup, giving that metallic sound that Jeff Beck remembers in Chicago blues.

The other point was that for the Chicago players they were using the clean sound on their amplifiers, which also contributed to the Chicago sound. The Fender Telecaster and the Fender Stratocaster had become quite popular guitars, but it was Eric Clapton's use of the Gibson Les Paul that was to make it so popular with blues guitarists.

Also around this time Eric got himself a new amplification set-up, which had been manufactured by an Englishman Jim Marshall. The output of this amp was 45 watts and it had a separate speaker cabinet with two twelve-inch speakers in it. Eric Clapton plugged his new Les Paul in to his new Marshall amp set-up and played with the amp turned full up; thus in one moment Eric Clapton created the rock guitar sound that was subsequently to be used by virtually every new rock group of the late sixties and early seventies.

Prior to this amplifier, guitar had sounded very different and subsequently Eric's guitar sound was to be an influence on some of the original black guitarists whom he most admired such as Freddie King, B.B. King and Buddy Guy. They all eventually began to play louder and with more sustain. If you don't believe me, check out their fifties recordings and then some of the recordings they made post-Clapton and the Bluesbreakers.

So back to the plot...

Clapton was in and Roger Dean was out. But unfortunately John Mayall didn't have a record contract. Enter stage left a white knight to save the day...

Chapter 14

Mike Vernon:
Record producer and visionary

Mike Vernon was a staff producer for Decca Records. He had followed down the same path as people like Bradford, having been introduced to the blues through the playing of Howlin' Wolf and Little Walter. A friend of his had lent him records of Little Walter performing 'My Babe And Juke' and Howlin' Wolf doing 'Smokestack Lightenin'. He also got hold of a Muddy Waters album. Mike Vernon remembers...

'Those records turned me on immediately to the blues. You see I had been buying Fats Domino's and Little Richard's records, which were rhythm and blues records. I thought they were rock 'n' roll records, but of course they were really blues records. From the moment that I was introduced to the blues, I never really looked back and I started buying a whole pile of the stuff.'

Mike had been given a job at Decca by Frank Lee. He started off as Frank Lee's lackey, running errands to the post office, making tea and answering the telephone. However, he eventually gained experience of the music business by working in every department including copyright, publishing, mastering, publicity and sleaving information. But it was record production in which Mike Vernon was interested.

Finally, he plucked up the courage to suggest to Frank Lee that Decca record a Texas blues singer and pianist that he had recently seen called Curtis Jones. He told Lee that he thought he could do it in a day. The record was released as *Curtis Jones In London*. It received a very good review in *Melody Maker* from journalist Matt Jones, who was one of the earliest journalistic friends of the blues in Britain. This was the first album Vernon had ever produced and it was the start of his career.

During this time, Mike attended the club gigs of Cyril Davies and Blues Incorporated and he also saw, among others, the Rolling Stones. Mike Vernon realised that there was a growing blues scene in London and it was him who persuaded Decca Records that they were wrong to drop John Mayall from their roster, most especially because of the fact that Eric Clapton had now joined the band.

John Mayall had become a little disillusioned with Decca, but Mike Vernon was able to persuade him to re-join because he convinced Mayall that Decca was one of the only record companies around that had people working for it that knew anything about the blues. Mayall responded and was prepared to sign the deal if it could be organised. The next thing that happened was a recording of the legendary Bluesbreakers album featuring Eric Clapton.

Chapter 15

The album... John Mayall's Bluesbreakers Featuring Eric Clapton

S hortly after joining John Mayall's Bluesbreakers, Eric Clapton was given a tiny room in John Mayall's house. John was living there with his family and Clapton, although he felt odd about being there, was given access to John Mayall's vast collection of blues records.

Now we come to one of the extraordinary qualities of John Mayall – and that is the fact that he was prepared to work with musicians who were almost twelve or thirteen years younger than himself.

Prior to that time the Rolling Stones had had to find their own spaces to play in the suburbs of London because the older established bands such as Cyril Davies' and Alexis Korner's had the whole scene sewn up. Cyril Davies, as Geoff Bradford remembers, did not think much of the Rolling Stones or of the Yardbirds. This is where that musical snobbery comes back into play. You see, as far as Cyril – as a self-appointed purist – was concerned, the Rolling Stones and the Yardbirds couldn't hack it as real blues players. This discrimination is something that Mick Jagger remembers to this day and it must have stung the ego at the time.

Therefore, it is all the more strange that John Mayall should have let the young Clapton into his band. It showed vision as well as being out and out opportunism since, when Eric's following from the Yardbirds had started to turn up at John Mayall gigs, Mayall was quick to spot the advantages. Eric Clapton remembers this about John Mayall:

'He was very good in that he would listen to me about music. He was one of the first people apart from Ben [Palmer] who did. We would listen to lots of blues and pick songs that were right for the stage. He was easy company and older than me, but keen to draw me out and find out what I thought. It was most unusual. A very important band for me. I did flower a lot during my time with Mayall.'

Most of Clapton's contemporaries age-wise were, at this time, in the early stages of forming pop bands or rock 'n' roll groups, based on the playing of Little Richard, Elvis Presley, Jerry Lee Lewis and Buddy Holly, as well as on such blues performers as Jerry Reed, Muddy Waters and Howlin' Wolf.

These younger bands such as the Who and the Rolling Stones were already beginning to fuse rhythm and blues with rock 'n' roll and other musical strains such as folk-song in to what was to become British rock music. Eventually this was a path that Eric Clapton was to go down himself.

The relationship between John Mayall and Eric Clapton was very complex. It was also full of tension from the start. Eric Clapton, as we have seen, was a very moody character and had a tendency to pick holes in any situation he found himself in. Eric Clapton remembers:

'I have always found something that isn't right. In that band it became John Mayall himself. With a couple of other members of the band we started to gang up on John behind his back, muttering about him not being a good enough singer and being too flamboyant in his presentation.'

This criticism of Mayall by Clapton is easy to understand when you consider that up until this time Eric had always virtually stood still on the stage to play his guitar, adopting a somewhat serious pose. As I remember it myself, he always appeared to be in a world of his own, somewhat separated from the rest of the group. Sometimes tension within a group is a good thing and although Eric Clapton did not remain for long with John Mayall's Bluesbreakers, the tension between Clapton and his band leader seems to have contributed in some way to the aggression that we hear in Clapton's guitar solos of the time. Being a perfectionist, Eric was never going to be happy with anything he played. He never was, and he never will be.

Having known both Geoff Bradford and Peter Green quite well, I can tell you that Eric's perspective was in no way unique. When I first started to record Geoff Bradford in the early seventies, I vividly remember one session we did together. Geoff had gone into the studio and sat down to record a track called 'Going Down Slow'. This was a solo guitar and vocal performance by Geoff. Geoff was on such brilliant form at that time; it was my practice simply to leave the tape machine running so as to capture the moment.

Geoff sat there and proceeded to do five versions, one after another, of the same song asking me each time what I thought and then promptly ignoring my reply and carrying on with his next version. As the record's producer I was forced to call and end to this. In the end I simply stopped the tape, got Geoff into the control room and told him:

'All these versions are fantastic and since you can't make up your mind, Geoff, I will choose one for myself.'

This seemed to work well and I have used this method ever since whenever I have worked with Geoff Bradford. I also heard a really interesting story about Peter Green from those times. Apparently, Peter would turn up at the studio, but if things didn't feel right once he had started playing he would immediately take a break or even go home and try again later.

I doubt that even though these great guitar players knew what they were after they had any idea of the kind of impression that their playing was making on their young contemporaries in the audience. After all, how could they ever be as good as their heroes? They were just not worthy.

Prior to recording with John Mayall's Bluesbreakers, Eric Clapton was touring with the group, playing a never-ending series of one night shows. Eric Clapton remembers...

'Mayall was amazing, I mean no one was allowed to drink! John McVie got slung out of the bandwagon half way between Birmingham and London on one occasion because he was drunk. He had to make his own way home. Also John had his own bunk bed in the van and you had to sit upright while he got into his bed and went to sleep.'

So obviously this emphasises the employer/employee relationship that Geoff Bradford remembers so well with Cyril Davies. At the end of the week Eric Clapton would get his £20 pay packet just like all the others in the group. John Mayall looked after everything else. He was the boss and it was his band.

By the summer of 1965, Eric Clapton had had enough of John Mayall's Bluesbreakers and decided to go off to Greece with a bunch of friends. John Mayall recalls:

'Eric was always a restless musician and I guess he just got bored with an endless session of one nighters. He just wanted to go away and abandon it. Of course, for me it was panic stations because we came to rely on him and there were so few people to choose from as a replacement. We got countless replies from a Melody Maker *advert – none of whom were it. I had Jeff Kribbett from Dr K's Bluesband for a while and during*

the weeks he was with me this other bloke kept coming up
saying: "I'm much better than him, why don't you use me." In
the end he got quite vicious about it and so I got him in and he
was better, and that was Peter Green. But three days later Eric
came back again from Greece and I had promised him his job
back if he ever came to his senses. So when he came back he
was back in the group, which didn't make Peter Green very
happy at all.'

John Mayall had the habit of occasionally recording gigs for his own
reference on a reel-to-reel tape recorder and it was thus that we were
able to hear Clapton's playing in the live context. His solo on the live
version of Muddy Waters' 'Hoochie Coochie Man' captures for all time
just what a revelation he was. Clapton's aggression, sense of timing and
the pure emotion that he was able to transmit in those days, have never
really been equalled by his subsequent performances. It was round
about that time that 'Clapton is God' started to appear spray-painted
on walls all over London. Later, Eric was to admit that secretly he
thought that the compliment, although completely over the top, was
well earned since he felt he had worked hard to become the best – and
he was. Eric is the first to admit that during this period he was perhaps
playing his best lead guitar. It's interesting to compare Eric's playing on
his recent album *From The Cradle* with the work he did while in the
Bluesbreakers. John Mayall sees it in this way:

'There's a lot of bullshit written about Eric leaving the blues all
these years. I don't see it that way. Eric is one of the all-time
genius guitar players and he can do no wrong. Every album he
has ever made is a big turn on to me because I don't hear
anything that isn't blues in his playing. Still From The Cradle *is*
very satisfying. Playing those old tunes is like a nostalgic trip.
We listened to those records at my house in the early days when
we were woodshedding in the Bluesbreakers. He'd say: "Hey,
listen to this Otis Rush one. Dig this Jimmy Rogers one." They

117

*would be obscure things to most people, but I had those records
and Eric and I used to listen to them.'*

The Bluesbreakers album featuring Eric Clapton has this famous
photograph for a front cover. The rest of the band are sitting on a low
bench looking straight at the camera. Behind them is a paint splattered
wall. Eric Clapton, however, is sitting reading a copy of a child's comic
called *The Beano*. Visually even this photograph singles Eric out as
being apart from the group.

This album was released in July 1966 and marks a watershed in the
development of the rock music art form. Let's look at that for a while.

Up until this time pop music, or young people's music, had not
been treated seriously by the 'establishment'. It was just something
that parents came to realise in the fifties and early sixties that they had
to tolerate until their beloved children settled down to raise families,
create children of their own. In some ways it's easy to understand just
what a threat Elvis Presley and the Beatles – let alone the Rolling Stones
– posed to the average parents' sense of security. After all, the songs of
this new generation of performers alluded to sex and a way of carrying
on that was outside of the accepted behaviour of 'normal people'. The
Rolling Stones looked like the kind of boys you most didn't want your
sons to end up looking like or your daughters to go out with. If you had
to settle for anybody you would much rather your son ended up
looking like one of the Beatles with their nice smart suits and hair cuts
than one of those unspeakable Rolling Stones.

It was the Rolling Stones who were the first of the counter culture
bands to get any kind of exposure on prime-time television, and their
appearance plus the on-stage performance of Mick Jagger was a cause
of much parental protest. However, being cast in the role of rebels
immediately endeared them to the younger generation. As we move
towards the middle of the decade the Rolling Stones, the Beatles and
the other new groups that were beginning to emerge found to their
great surprise that their appeal to their peers had an unforeseen
staying power. Geoff Bradford remembers...

'When I was playing on the scene I didn't think the music was gonna last at all. At that time none of us – Alexis, Cyril or me – saw the scene as being anything other than a load of blues enthusiasts playing to an audience of fellow enthusiasts. Musicians would come and go and the whole scene was very fluid. When Brian Jones asked me to start rehearsing with the early Rolling Stones, I had no idea about what was to follow. To me he was just a young slide guitar player with a load of enthusiasm. At that time I would play with virtually anyone who gave me a chance to play guitar. That was my passion, playing the guitar, and to me it didn't matter if it was Brian Jones, Brian Knight, Cyril Davies or Alexis Korner.

'I often used to deputise for Alexis Korner when he used to book himself out for different venues on the same night. What he would do was simply play the best gig that night and get me to play the other one. I remember on one occasion getting an emergency call from Alexis asking me to deputise for him at the Ealing Club. I got on the bus with my guitar and left my little amplifier downstairs in the compartment for luggage that was under the stairs of the London Transport double-decker I was riding on. This was just your average public London bus, you know the kind they put on the front of American tourist brochures.

'I arrived at the Ealing Club to find Jack Bruce and Ginger Baker glaring at me. They were both in a foul temper, but it was a great gig. That was typical of the kind of thing that went on all the time in those days but none of us had any idea that the whole scene would take off. The point was that when the Beatles came out we all felt that we were as far away from that kind of pop music as we were from Cliff Richard and the Shadows, and Marty Wilde, and Gerry and the Pacemakers. I'll tell you this though: I saw the Rolling Stones right at the beginning at a little club gig they were doing – it might even have been an unofficial rehearsal. I went down just to look. I was curious having played with them

earlier on and I can tell you that they were really good and I was very impressed, especially with Jagger's energy. The point is everything seemed to move on so quickly – and that was the same with Eric Clapton's guitar playing.'

In 1966, the Bluesbreakers album was released alongside records such as *Aftermath* by the Rolling Stones, *Pet Sounds* by the Beachboys, *Blonde On Blonde* by Bob Dylan and *Revolver* by the Beatles. These records were much more than pop and since the LP record format was beginning to outsell singles and EPs a new culture of rock music was beginning to be established.

Rock music combines the meaningful lyrics of folk-songs with the power and energy of rhythm and blues and the sexiness of rock 'n' roll. British rock music has always been fusion music and nobody really does this better. Bands like Dire Straits and U2 are still doing this even today.

The release in 1966 of *John Mayall's Bluesbreakers Featuring Eric Clapton* gave the world its first white virtuoso rock guitar soloist, and to many Eric Clapton's playing on that record has never been equalled from the point of view of aggression and attack. Clapton was rapidly to take this new rock blues guitar soloing technique into Cream.

After the success of *John Mayall's Bluesbreakers Featuring Eric Clapton*, Clapton was propelled through to stardom in a far wider context. The Bluesbreakers album along with all the other LPs released during 1966, began to emphasise studio sophistication and technique against the package tours and singles that had been the daily grind of performers up until that time.

John Mayall's open-door policy and his willingness to nurture and bring through a younger man's talent had given Eric Clapton, this passionate and slightly disturbed young man, a vehicle through which to display his undoubted musical talents. Nobody was expecting what happened next.

While Eric Clapton had been away in the summer of 1965 on that trip to Greece, John McVie had been temporarily thrown out of the band by John Mayall for excessive boozing. John Mayall invited Jack Bruce, a fiery Scottish bass player who was a veteran of Alexis Korner's Blues Incorporated and of the Graham Bond Organisation, to join the Bluesbreakers.

The Graham Bond Organisation was a spin-off band from Alexis Korner's Blues Incorporated. Sax and keyboard player Graham Bond, had formed a group with ex-Blues Incorporated drummer Ginger Baker and bass player Jack Bruce. After Cyril Davies had split up with Alexis Korner a big gap had been left in Blues Incorporated. Alexis needed to find some kind of replacement for Cyril. (Alexis, you will remember, was more interested in pursuing a jazz-based form of blues, whereas Cyril Davies was far more interested in the hard blues of Chicago South Side.)

Alexis found his replacement in Graham Bond, who was a very talented instrumentalist. He was an alto sax player as well as a keyboard player and had been voted 'Britain's New Jazz Star' when he had been playing with the Don Rendell Quintet in 1961.

Graham Bond turned out to be an excellent choice. He had some of the physical presence of Cyril Davies and his Hammond Lesley organ sound, as well as his singing and sax playing, filled the hole left by the departure of Cyril Davies, who had also taken with him another of Blues Incorporated vocalists, Long John Baldry. With Jack Bruce on bass and Ginger Baker on drums, along with Graham Bond on keyboards, the new Blues Incorporated rhythm section represented a major force. They rapidly added another sax player to the line up – Dick Heckstall-Smith. Inevitably, as was the tradition of the time, this line up did not last for long before Graham Bond decided to make his own way, taking Jack Bruce and Ginger Baker with him.

Jack Bruce and Ginger Baker had a very fiery relationship during this time and eventually Baker was to sack Bruce from the band having taken over the running of the group because he didn't seem to be getting enough money from Graham Bond. However, Jack Bruce didn't seem to want to go and eventually Ginger Baker ended up threatening Jack Bruce with a knife. At this time Ginger Baker was a registered heroin addict.

By June 1966, Ginger Baker was beginning to get fed up with playing in the Graham Bond Organisation. Graham Bond's behaviour on and off stage was becoming increasingly erratic. Ginger Baker unexpectedly turned up at a Bluesbreakers gig in Oxford and suggested that he sat in on the drums. Mayall's drummer, Hughie Flint, had no objections to this since he was a fan of Ginger Baker.

After this Ginger Baker began turning up at other gigs. Eventually, Ginger suggested to Eric that they might form a group together and Eric Clapton, who received the idea enthusiastically since he wasn't happy with the John Mayall situation, suggested Jack Bruce. This was somewhat ironic when you consider the clash between Jack Bruce and Ginger Baker in the Graham Bond Organisation, but as much because of Eric Clapton's status, Ginger Baker agreed.

Jack Bruce joined John Mayall's Bluesbreakers during the short period that Eric Clapton was away. Jack Bruce says...

'When Eric got back from Greece, the first gig we did together was at London Airport. There used to be a gig at the airport for the staff. When Eric started to play I had never heard anything like it before. I think he had seen and heard me with the Graham Bond Organisation, but I had never seen him before. We had an instant rapport which led us to having long chats about what our hopes and aims were. I thought that although the blues was great there was more than that. It was a beginning rather than an end. Anyway, I left John Mayall for financial reasons as much as anything else. I had only been married a short time and I was trying to pay the rent and eat. I had scuffled [led the hard life] enough.'

Jack Bruce left John Mayall to take up a more lucrative offer from Manfred Mann. (This was to result in a track on the *Bluesbreakers featuring Eric Clapton* album called 'Double Crossing Time', which was a reference to Bruce's departure. The composition of this track is credited to John Mayall and Eric Clapton.)

Manfred Mann, with their lead singer Paul Jones, had become a successful pop band of the time with such hits as 'Five, Four, Three, Two, One', which was used as the title music for the very successful and influential television music show *Ready, Steady, Go!*, which was a feature of the London scene at the time. Anyway, by that time Eric Clapton had become a very erratic member of John Mayall's Bluesbreakers, often not turning up for gigs at all. Jack Bruce having previously left John Mayall's band just before the recording of the classic *Bluesbreakers featuring Eric Clapton* album, decided that although playing with Manfred Mann paid well, musically it did not provide much satisfaction. And so Cream were formed in or around July 1966. The original idea, which was Eric Clapton's, was that the band should be like the Buddy Guy Bluesband. However, once they got going it soon evolved in to a more surreal outfit. John Mayall asked John McVie to re-join the Bluesbreakers and it was with this line up that the classic *Bluesbreakers* album was recorded.

Having left once for Greece, Eric Clapton finally departed from the Bluesbreakers in July 1966. This was exactly the same month as the *Bluesbreakers featuring Eric Clapton* album was released by Decca – which really left John Mayall in serious trouble. The album reached No. 6 in the UK charts and represented for John Mayall his first real success – and obviously he was keen to get out there and exploit the situation through live gigging. It was thus that Mayall asked Peter Green to join the band. However, Peter took quite a lot of persuasion having already been rejected once by John Mayall in favour of the returning Eric Clapton. He also had an offer from another R&B-based band called the Animals. Eventually, he accepted Mayall's offer.

During his term with the Bluesbreakers, Eric Clapton was encouraged to sing by John Mayall. This is not something he was very happy about and significantly he was to record a Robert Johnson track for Mayall called 'Rambling On My Mind'. Clapton, remember, was a major Johnson fan and since those days Clapton's vocal performance has gone from strength to strength; on his recent album *From The*

Cradle plus his biggest selling release *Unplugged*, his voice is as much a feature of his performance as his guitar playing.

Peter Green, who now took over the role of lead guitar player from Eric Clapton, was already a good singer, and it was while with John Mayall that he also started to write his own songs.

Chapter 16

John Mayall with Peter Green...
A hard road

P eter Green had an entirely different personality to Eric Clapton. He was ambitious, confident of his own abilities, laid back and far easier to work with than Clapton had been.

He was very happy to have got the job of replacing Clapton in Mayall's band because he realised that this meant almost instant stardom, even though this would be limited to the London blues scene.

At this point we need to break off from our main story line once again, to examine the second phase of the London blues boom...

During 1965 and through 1966, other blues-based bands were beginning to come together. Such bands as Ten Years After, Chicken Shack, Savoy Brown and Jethro Tull began to arrive on the scene, which really started to take off again during 1967.

The success of Cream was also a major factor in popularising the blues to an even larger audience and by this time, mid-1967, Jimi Hendrix was also in London.

In 1967, I was seventeen years old and, as you will remember, had just moved to Richmond, Surrey – and to a large extent it was people of my age or slightly older who were to form a substantial part of the new audience. The audience was mostly male and the standard wear of the time was long overcoats, jeans and baseball boots, as well as rugby shirts, which were becoming popular. This was a kind of uniform and everyone had long hair. It was around this time that the term 'the underground' came in to use to describe this set of people.

What we have here is another counter culture, which spurned the pop single market and concentrated more and more on buying albums (long playing records). Another thing about this audience was that it was better informed regarding the blues and rhythm and blues, since many more American performers had become available in the UK on record.

The take-off point for this scene was the *Windsor Blues Festival* of August 1967, which featured John Mayall, Cream, Jeff Beck, Ten Years After, Chicken Shack and last, but by no means least, perhaps the most successful blues band of all time to emerge from the London scene... Fleetwood Mac.

OK. Back to the plot!

Peter Green joined John Mayall's Bluesbreakers in July 1966 and he left in May 1967, so like Eric Clapton he wasn't in the group for very long. One can only imagine how it must have been for Peter Green. Eric Clapton had established a huge reputation among the blues community as an outstanding lead guitarist and just before what was to turn out to be a classic album release, he left John Mayall! So Peter Green was immediately thrust into Eric Clapton's shoes.

There are varying opinions from this time as to audience reaction to Mayall's new young lead guitar player. This is what Peter told me when I interviewed him. I should add that I had many, many conversations with Peter Green when he lived in Richmond. Basically, this is his story...

'When I started off with John Mayall I was trying to cover for Eric Clapton. So therefore I used to overplay a lot, at least to my

way of thinking. From the start I didn't play things like 'Hideaway', but I did do another Freddie King instrumental called 'The Stumble'. Having got to know John Mayall I was able to sit and listen to his vast collection of blues records. I remember we used to listen to J.B. Lenoir a lot, who was one of John's heroes.'

Peter also said this about trying to fill Eric Clapton's shoes:

'Well, I was kind of being everything. I was jumping the gun a bit; I was trying to play as good as Eric Clapton. I had to try it, because I had to fill his place.'

In many ways Peter Green was far more the blues man than Eric Clapton ever was or ever would be. For a start, he had a great singing voice and also as a guitarist he seemed to be playing within the music, or even behind the music, rather than dominating it from the front – which was what Eric Clapton was clearly doing.

There's a track that was re-issued later on by Decca from that live recording which John Mayall had done featuring Eric Clapton on lead guitar. It's really the instrumental introduction to 'Stormy Monday Blues'. On this live track, which is recorded very much in lo-fi rather than hi-fi, Eric's guitar is almost incendiary. He literally blows the place to pieces. His sense of timing and phrasing, as well as his out and out attack, is a pointer to the kind of playing that he would shortly produce in Cream without any of the latter band's excesses.

In my interview with Peter Green, I asked him how he got into blues guitar in the first place. He laughed and simply said: 'Eric Clapton!'. He went on to tell me that he had seen Eric play in the Yardbirds and he had thought that he could 'come alongside' him in some way. I asked him what he meant by this and he said:

'Well, you know how good he was... Well, the whole thing was that there was heart there, there was generosity there, there was a good person there.'

I then asked him whether he meant by 'come alongside' that he would play in the same way as Eric. He answered:

'No, I could turn people on with a note of sadness. With a note of sadness, I maybe could do that. Like Sachmo, you know that kind of feeling, well Eric Clapton could do it as well and John Mayall could do it. Aretha Franklin, the Staples Singers, all these people I started hearing. J.B. Lenoir is like the master of it, but Eric Clapton did kind of do something like that. He didn't really do what J.B. Lenoir does, but he did something and it might have coincided with something of mine, but it's not such a big inspiration. I actually took over the group. I ended up taking over the group he left.'

During his time with John Mayall, and as a result of John Mayall's enthusiasm and support, Peter Green began to experiment with writing his own songs. One of these compositions, 'The Same Way', was to appear on the *Hard Road* album. Another song that Peter wrote while he was hanging out in John Mayall's house was to become world famous when it was a hit for Santana. This was 'Black Magic Woman'. Peter told me:

'I wrote it when I was with John Mayall, I was living in John Mayall's house when I started to write that. I write songs in bits and pieces. John Mayall started me writing blues things. He said to me what I could do was what he does sometimes. If he hadn't done it first I wouldn't have done it because it's a strange thing to do really. To take the first line or the last line of something and to write a song like another song. If you're playing a song, someone else's song, and if you really, really like it, if you're bubbling over with it, then you should take – it must be the first line, because I did that thing 'Merry-Go-Round', which is a copy of 'Sweet Sixteen', B.B. King's 'Sweet Sixteen'.

So I asked if that's what he did with 'Black Magic Woman'. And Peter said:

'Yeah, I took something out of 'All Your Love', but it wasn't really like 'All Your Love' in the end, it was like 'Help The Poor' by B.B. King.'

Once again back to the plot... So here we are just at the point when the Eric Clapton/John Mayall combination is about to take off – and Eric leaves. So imagine if you can how that record's producer, Mike Vernon, and studio engineer, Gus Dudgeon, felt when John Mayall arrived for his next recording sessions at Decca's West Hampstead studios.

Mayall had neglected to inform these two about Eric Clapton's departure. When Mayall broke the news to them they were slightly put out and even more so when Mayall introduced Peter Green to them as the new guitarist who was going to fill Eric's shoes, claiming: 'Don't worry, we have got somebody better!'. Mike Vernon remembers:

'I said: "Wait a minute, hang on a second, this is ridiculous. You have got a replacement? You have got somebody better? than Eric Clapton. I find that hard to believe."'

John Mayall's answer gives a really clear indication of just what a visionary he really was. He said:

'He may not be better right now, but you wait... in a couple of years he's going to be the best.'

Then John Mayall introduced Mike Vernon to Peter Green. A short time after this, when Peter Green had left John Mayall's Bluesbreakers, it was Mike Vernon who was to suggest to Peter that he form his own band; it was also Mike Vernon who was to sign Fleetwood Mac, Peter's new band, to his own new blues record label called Blue Horizon. It was Mike Vernon who, Peter Green reminded me, 'introduced me to

Jeremy Spencer'.

Once Peter Green was in John Mayall's Bluesbreakers he started touring round with the band playing the normal Mayall gig schedule of one nighters. At first, because Eric Clapton had taken his audience with him, attendance at these gigs was reduced. Hughie Flint had become more and more disillusioned with the situation. Eventually Flint was to get 'that phone call' from John Mayall: 'Hello, I've got a new drummer!'.

Before leaving though, Hughie Flint was asked to play a few more engagements that had already been booked. At the end of these, John Mayall paid Hughie a reduced wage due apparently, he said, to the fact that audiences had tailed off a bit since Eric had left. Now to me that sounds like a bit of a cheek to put it mildly, and it was from moves like this that John Mayall was to get his reputation as a hard taskmaster. Definitely an employee/employer relationship working here, wouldn't you say?

Hughie Flint was replaced by a young drummer from Liverpool called Aynsley Dunbar, who had played with the Merseysippi Jazz Band and ended up in London playing with Stu James and the Mojos.

The departure of Hughie Flint – John Mayall's longest serving drummer at twenty-nine months – marked the beginning of the disintegration of the classic Bluesbreakers rhythm section of John Mayall on keyboards and rhythm guitar, John McVie on bass and Hughie Flint on drums.

The new line up, which featured Peter Green on lead guitar, John Mayall on vocals and keyboard, John McVie on bass and Aynsley Dunbar on drums, was not to last long. However, they did record the Bluesbreakers second classic album, *A Hard Road*, which was released in February 1967. It reached No. 10 in the UK charts.

Once this new line up began to gig, Peter Green and John McVie, who had by this time formed quite a close friendship, began to feel that Aynsley Dunbar's drumming was too ornate and not what was really required for a blues band.

To add insult to injury, Dunbar would occasionally demand to take drum solos, which left McVie and Green standing and watching on the stage. This is something that Peter Green especially did not like. So inevitably Aynsley Dunbar left.

He was replaced for a few gigs by Mickey Waller (who had previously played with Cyril Davies' Allstars), but then he in turn was replaced by an old friend of Peter Green's, Mick Fleetwood, who you remember Peter had played with in Peter Bardens' group Peter B's Looners, who subsequently changed their name to Shotgun Express. Mick Fleetwood was fired after a month for getting drunk too many times, which was the ultimate sin as far as teetotaller John Mayall was concerned.

In another of a seemingly endless stream of ironies, as a birthday present John Mayall gave Peter Green some studio time. Peter went into the studio with Mick Fleetwood and John McVie and cut an instrumental track which they called 'Fleetwood Mac' – and thus we see the first mention of the band name that was to become, eventually, one of the biggest record-selling musical units of all time.

With Peter Green gaining in confidence all the time as a singer, a writer and a guitarist, it wasn't long before he decided to move on and form his own band. He really wanted to take John McVie with him so that they could join up with Mick Fleetwood, but McVie was reluctant to leave the financial security of John Mayall's Bluesbreakers.

Now we come to a really funny story...

Peter Green, as was the regular practice of the time when you were looking for a new musician, put an advert in *Melody Maker*'s Musicians Wanted section. He got a reply from a bass player called Bob Brunning who turned up at Green's flat in Putney. Bob Brunning remembers:

'I'd spotted an advert in Melody Maker *which simply read... "Bass player wanted for Chicago-type blues band" followed by a number, which I called. It proved to be a wrong number due to a misprint, but a hunch told me to pursue it, and I called the paper to get the correct one. I got through and arranged to audition. I went along with my old friend Martyn Yates for moral support, and turned up at a South London Council flat in Putney. I was greeted by a guy who introduced himself as*

Peter Green. I had heard about a brilliant successor to Eric Clapton who was playing in the current John Mayall band, called Peter Green although I hadn't seen the band. So I said to him: "You've certainly got the right name for a blues guitarist. Do you know about your namesake who plays with John Mayall?" to which Peter Green replied: "You bloody idiot, I am Peter Green."'

What a great story this is and what a great man Bob Brunning is for making it public so that we can all enjoy it. There are many people that I have met along the way that would wish to forget such an embarrassing moment.

Despite this, though, Bob Brunning was given the job as bass player and appeared with Fleetwood Mac at their first gig in 1967 at the *Windsor Blues Festival*. He was later replaced, as we will see, by John McVie, who in all fairness had been Mick Fleetwood's and Peter Green's first choice. This changeover came about as follows.

John McVie was still with the Bluesbreakers, but John Mayall was back with the same old problem. He had now lost a second star guitar player. At this point he decided to change direction. The decision involved adding two saxophone players to the band – Chris Mercer and Rip Kant. These were both session men who had played with John Mayall on earlier Bluesbreaker albums. This change of direction was too much for John McVie, who still considered himself to be an out and out blues musician, so having recorded one more album – *Crusade* – with John Mayall and the Bluesbreakers, he left and called Peter Green, accepting his offer to join Fleetwood Mac. John McVie had been the longest serving Mayall side-man, clocking in at fifty-six months. This decision finally ended what, for me – and for most other blues fans – was the classic Bluesbreakers period.

With the departure of John McVie, the Bluesbreakers were thrown into turmoil. Peter Green was replaced by a young guitarist who had been playing in a band from Hatfield in Hertfordshire called the Gods. At one time along the way, on one of the nights when Eric Clapton didn't show up, this young guitarist jumped up on stage and played with John Mayall and had then promptly disappeared.

But Mayall, in typical style, had logged the potential of this guitarist in some part of his brain and now set about trying to find him. In the end it was back to the Musicians Wanted page of the *Melody Maker*, and sure enough eventually Mick Taylor got in touch. He was nineteen when he joined John Mayall in June 1967, by which time John Mayall was thirty-four years old.

The new line up went straight into the studio to record the Bluesbreakers fourth album called *Crusade*, released 1 September, 1967. This is what John Mayall had to say about the new album in the sleeve note that he wrote for it at the time:

'You will see many new faces here now. Alongside John McVie and myself you will see Mick Taylor on guitar, Keef Hartley on drums, Chris Mercer on tenor sax and Rip Kant on baritone sax. These are the new Bluesbreakers and I hope you will appreciate their work as much as I appreciate them all as people. I will not speak here of their individual talent, but will let you hear this record and leave their appraisal to you.

'A word or two about the choice of material: I have chosen to campaign for some of my blues heroes by recording one number each from their own recorded repertoires and, amongst the original compositions, I include a tribute to J. B. Lenoir whose untimely death came as a great shock to me. I was even more saddened by the fact that his death only rated a couple of brief paragraphs in one British musical paper and it seems that his short life was one of great work without reward. It is about time that the blues fraternity made an outcry against a system locked in the belief that blues fans are only a small minority in the world of popular music. Hence the title of this new Bluesbreakers LP – Crusade*. I have dedicated my life to the blues... I hope you'll join forces with me.'*

Mick Taylor was to record three more albums with John Mayall: *Diary Of A Band* (Volumes I and II), *Bare Wires* and finally *Blues From*

Laurel Canyon.

In May 1969, Mick Taylor left John Mayall to join the Rolling Stones. As with Eric Clapton and Peter Green, Taylor had grown during his time as a Bluesbreaker. After 14 July, 1968 John Mayall stopped using the term 'Bluesbreakers'. He said at the time:

'This was a result of my decision to work more in a solo capacity with a small backing group. This boiled down to choosing the right personnel for the new quartet formation. I doubt if there could have been a better choice than Mick Taylor who really shows his brilliance on this new album.'

The album he is referring to is *Blues From Laurel Canyon*, which features a set of songs – all composed by John Mayall – documenting a trip that Mayall had made to Laurel Canyon in California. Shortly after this, John Mayall left the UK and took up permanent residence in the USA in December 1970.

I have always loved the guitar playing of Mick Taylor both as a lead guitarist and as a slide lead guitarist, and remember well spending many hours listening to *Blues From Laurel Canyon*, which was one of my favourite LPs at the time. Released in December 1968, it reached number No. 68 in the US chart and pointed the way to an ever increasing awareness by the US audience of John Mayall.

In 1971, John Mayall contacted many of the musicians that he had worked with during the sixties and recorded an album entitled *Back To The Roots*, which featured contributions from both Eric Clapton and Mick Taylor.

Here's a typical Eric Clapton comment summing up his period in John Mayall's band. As ever with Eric Clapton, you can never quite tell where the irony ends and the truth begins, but here it is anyway.

'Mayall had to be the one band where I really felt most at home. Poor old John; everyone takes the mickey out of him, but when you look at it, he's actually run an incredibly great school for musicians. I mean, most of the people that have gone through his school have turned out pretty well, you know!'

Part II

Chapter 17

Blues into rock:
An overview and the John
Mayall connection

The classic bluesbreaker period that produced John Mayall's two albums *Bluesbreakers featuring Eric Clapton* and *A Hard Road* stand at a junction point in the development of British rock music. In this second part of this book, I intend to look at the wider picture with regard to the development of pop music in this country and to try to place into context the blues scene and also to highlight the moment when British blues mutated into progressive rock. Over the years British rock music has dominated the world and produced some of the finest moments of rock music history. Many of the factors, both musical and in the development of studio technology, took place at the same time as the Bluesbreakers classic recordings.

The development of popular American music has had an effect on the development of the English scene, but equally the British have been immensely influential on the Americans, so in this section we will make an attempt to put it all together.

In the mid-1990s, the blues continues to crop up everywhere and to some extent its influence is more extensive than ever before. A major factor in this, of course, has been the arrival of a new recording medium, the digital compact disc. This has caused the biggest revolution of all as far as making the blues available is concerned and it's true to say that for a young musician growing up in our times he or she has access to the history of both white and black blues that would have been the envy of all those *blues purists* who were on the early London blues scene.

Fleetwood Mac

After leaving John Mayall's Bluesbreakers, Peter Green formed Fleetwood Mac in April 1967. During the time that Peter was in Bluesbreakers, producer Mike Vernon had used the rhythm section plus Peter without John Mayall to back US blues man Eddie Boyd for his new Blue Horizon label. Mike Vernon was very keen to sign a blues band from the British side of the water and he had already been auditioning bands – including a Midlands band called the Levi Set.

This band included a young guitar player called Jeremy Spencer who was nineteen years old. Mike Vernon was not impressed with the band and rejected them. However, he was impressed with Spencer who had learnt the Elmore James songbook by heart. Elmore James, you will remember, was one of the inheritors of the Robert Johnson legacy and was famous as a singer and slide guitar player.

Mike Vernon introduced Jeremy Spencer to Peter Green and Mick Fleetwood and thus Fleetwood Mac was formed. The band consisted of Peter Green (guitar and vocals), Mick Fleetwood (drums), Jeremy Spencer (guitar and vocals) and temporary bass player Bob Brunning. As we have seen, Bob Brunning was soon to be replaced by John McVie. After leaving the band, Bob formed the Sunflower Blues Band.

Right from the start, even when Bob Brunning was still in the band, Fleetwood Mac were recording tracks such as 'Long Gray Mare' and 'Rambling Pony' in the middle of the night at Decca's West Hampstead studios. Mike Vernon remembers...

'Yes, extremely late at night in the big studio at Decca. We

138

shouldn't have been there and nobody at Decca knew what we were doing.'

It was with these tapes that Mike Vernon was able to secure a distribution deal for his new Blues Horizon records with the American based CBS Records.

Looking back at it now after almost thirty years, and having myself had many long conversations with Peter Green while he was living in Richmond, it was obvious right from the start of Fleetwood Mac that Peter's experience in John Mayall's Bluesbreakers was showing its effect. With Peter having had to step into Eric Clapton's shoes, John Mayall really had no option but to push him forward as a lead guitarist. The trouble was that Peter was filling the shoes of not just a lead guitarist, but of a 'star' lead guitarist.

Now at that time, Peter was very ambitious and jumped at this opportunity, but he was also in his own eyes a blues man. What this meant for Peter was that the overall sound of a blues performance was very important and the idea of being thrust forward within the context of the group as a star guitar player, un-nerved him. Thus we can see why he introduced Jeremy Spencer into the group. This allowed him to take a break from being the centre of attention, as Spencer could both sing and play his Elmore James copies.

Fleetwood Mac released their debut single 'I Believe My Time Ain't Long' on 3 November, 1967. On this single the band were billed as Peter Green's Fleetwood Mac. The reason for this is obvious: it was Peter who had gained a reputation from his playing with John Mayall's Bluesbreakers. But very soon the band were to drop Peter's name from the billing.

Fleetwood Mac also became the resident house band for the Blue Horizon label backing Otis Span, Duster Bennett and others on albums. Fleetwood Mac's debut album simply called *Peter Green's Fleetwood Mac* was released in March 1968 and made No. 4 in the UK album charts. This album had a cover that showed an alleyway with an old dustbin and a dog in it. Visually this somehow seemed to encapsulate the music that was to serve as a counterpoint to that of the other immediate Bluesbreakers progeny – Cream.

Fleetwood Mac's first album stayed in the UK charts for more than a year and in a poll conducted by *Melody Maker*, it was judged by its readers to be the second best album in 1968. The band began from the start to draw huge audiences.

It was in the early days of Fleetwood Mac that Peter Green's potential as a blues guitarist began to blossom, especially at live gigs. I saw both Peter Green in Fleetwood Mac and Eric Clapton in Cream at the time, and the difference between the two of them as guitarists really was profound. Eric was playing power solos, pushed on by the virtuoso rhythm section of Jack Bruce and Ginger Baker. The fact is that Ginger Baker and Jack Bruce, with their jazz backgrounds, had a complex inter-action that was propelling Eric's guitar playing, which was and always has been rooted in the blues into a totally new dimension.

Peter Green on the other hand, backed by his straight down the middle rhythm section of Fleetwood and McVie, was left in a far more exposed position musically. This had the effect of highlighting his guitar playing. Another factor that added to this was that when Jeremy Spencer came forward to play his Elmore James pieces the effect was virtually to turn the band into a band within a band. When Jeremy was singing and playing his slide, the group did sound quite like a Chicago South Side blues band. But when Peter sang and played there was always something else present that seemed to transcend the Chicago blues sound.

The first recorded evidence of this transition can be heard on the single 'Black Magic Woman' which, you will remember, Peter had started to write when still with John Mayall's Bluesbreakers. 'Black Magic Woman' was not an immediate hit for Fleetwood Mac, only reaching No. 37 in the UK charts. The song is in two parts: the first part highlights a beautiful interplay between Peter Green's voice and his guitar playing; the second part sees the band breaking into their well-known shuffle rhythm with Peter opening out on lead guitar, but playing beautifully controlled phrases.

The point of Peter Green's guitar playing was that it exploited the spaces between the notes as much as the notes themselves. Peter had that touch which meant that he was able to convey tremendous emotion through his guitar work.

In July 1968, Fleetwood Mac issued a single which was a version of Little Willie John's blues classic 'Need Your Love So Bad'. This track had a string arrangement by Mickey Baker. Mickey 'Guitar' Baker was a famous jazz player and had taken time out from working in Paris to write the string parts and conduct the orchestra – a fact that Peter considered to be a tremendous accolade.

B.B. King had done a version of this song and B.B. had been one of Peter's guitar influences. 'Black Magic Woman' and 'Need Your Love So Bad' represent Peter Green standing at his own crossroads. By this time his creativity as a composer, and his compelling voice were beginning to become as much a factor as his wonderful lead guitar playing. For me, 'Need Your Love So Bad' represents a high point in the history of British rock blues guitar. For sure you can hear elements of the playing of Shadows' guitarist Hank Marvin combining with the sweet tones of B.B. King. But by comparing Peter's playing on this track with those other two guitarists we can immediately see just how much is pure Peter Green.

In September 1968, the band released their second album, *Mr Wonderful*, which went to No. 10 in the UK charts. The album featured piano playing by Christine Perfect, who was later to marry bass player John McVie.

In December 1968, Fleetwood Mac released an instrumental written by Peter Green called 'Albatross'. This track was very much *not* a blues band track and launched Fleetwood Mac to a wider audience as it went to No. 1 in the UK charts. By this time Peter Green had added another guitarist to the band, eighteen year old Danny Kirwan. This can be seen as a further attempt by Peter to take pressure of himself by dividing the role of lead guitarist in three: Kirwan and Spencer (playing his slide guitar) and himself. However, the less Peter Green played on stage and on record, the more it became obvious just how unique his playing was.

Fleetwood Mac, during a break from touring in America, recorded some tracks at the famous Chess Studios in Chicago. These recordings were eventually released as *Blues Jam At Chess* so at last Peter got to record at the heart of a scene that had been such an inspiration to him as a musician.

Further Peter Green classic performances include 'Need Your Love So Bad', 'Oh Well' (which touched on religious subjects), 'Man Of The World' (the lyrics of which give a graphic description of Peter's state of mind) and finally 'The Green Manalishi (With The Two-Prong Crown)'. The power of 'The Green Manalishi' is awesome and Peter held nothing back in its performance. It is a true piece of rock music: it's not a blues, it's not a pop song, it's not rock 'n' roll and it definitely isn't folk music; it's a new kind of music, a fusion of many of the strands that had contributed to Peter Green's musical education. It was also Peter's swan-song. The lyrics, written by Peter, talk of his disillusionment with the whole business side of the music, which by that time had begun to become a larger and larger factor in his daily life. In the end this contradiction between blues man that he so obviously was at heart, and material wealth unbalanced him. He told me later that 'The Green Manalishi' was about green-backs (a slang word used in America to describe the dollar) and that the effect of material wealth was to bring you down. In the middle of the vocal Peter sings: '*You're the Green Manalishi with the two-prong crown/All my trying is up/All you're bringing is down/Busting in on my dreams making me see things I don't wanna see*'. Nothing more, I think, needs to be said and after recording this track Peter Green left Fleetwood Mac.

Peter's mental breakdown is a well documented fact, but you can read another view of this in Martin Clemins' biography of Peter Green. That book quotes from time to time from my interview with Peter, which I had recorded on tape on 5 September, 1984 and which was first published in *Guitarist* magazine in September 1993.

There are two reasons why I made this interview available to the

142

public. First and foremost was that I had read so much in the media that seemed to contradict the Peter Green I knew. I had originally done this interview as part of a series I was doing at the time which included folk guitar legend Bert Jansch and acoustic blues guitar virtuoso and singer (and great personal friend) Cliff Aungier.

I was beginning to see myself turning into a bit of an Alan Lomax/John Lomax figure. These two, as you will remember, had gone round interviewing and recording blues musicians for the Library of Congress and I thought I had better get some stuff on tape for posterity, which I did – but it was my private collection and the Peter Green interview sat on the shelf for nearly ten years.

The second reason that I allowed this interview to be published was entirely due to the integrity of two of the editors of *Guitarist*: Neville Marten and Eddie Allen – both of whom are very knowledgeable and dedicated to guitar music. They assured me the interview would be reproduced in *Guitarist* (the biggest selling guitar magazine in Europe) as it had been given to me by Peter. This they did to the letter.

Since that time, Gary Moore, a highly respected British guitarist has brought out an album that is entirely made up of Peter Green compositions. Gary Moore has had a lot of success in the nineties with a series of albums that feature his blues guitar sound. Just before Peter dropped out of the scene, he gave his Gibson Les Paul to Gary and Gary uses it on his CD, which is called *Blues For Greeney*; and as I write I am told there is a further tribute album being put together on Peter. Therefore I felt it right to publish in this book the whole text of my interview with Peter Green.

Both Gary Moore and myself share a great admiration for Peter and his playing, and wouldn't it be great if one day Peter decided to record again.

You grew up in the East End – Bethnal Green?
'Yes, the first part of my life.'

And you went to be a butcher's apprentice?
'In the end I didn't serve an apprenticeship, I just went as another

143

member of the shop. I wasn't good at it at all; I couldn't master it. There's a feeling that you had when you had mastered it, but I never got anything but, "No, that isn't right."'

Were you listening to music at the time?
'Yes, of course I was; anything that was coming to my ears.'

You liked the blues singer J.B. Lenoir, didn't you?
'I did hear J.B. Lenoir as a child. He is a very special symbol of African slavery. His singing is really symbolic, truthfully symbolic; it really puts you there because of the high voice.'

Did you listen to Hank Marvin?
Yes, loved it. Beautiful, very soothing. I find it very inoffensive.

And people like Freddie King and Buddy Guy; when did you start listening to them?
'After Eric Clapton. After I'd heard the Rolling Stones, the Yardbirds, John Lee Hooker, that kind of thing.'

Were they your inspiration to take up the guitar?
'No. It was just my brother. My brother was strumming and I said wished I could. And he gave me a chord book to see if I could pick anything up from it, but I couldn't. I didn't even recognise the chord that I could play already. I couldn't make anything of it.'

Did you find the guitar itself difficult to learn?
'Yes I did, now I think about it. My brother taught me the chords, but when he wasn't around I found it impossible to do anything but these chords. It was very hard for me to learn lead lines. I can see myself looking at the guitar neck, now, and I really didn't know what to make of it.'

How did you learn it in the end, then?
'Do you remember the programme Gun Law? *Well. I knew I could,
pick up those few notes, by trial and error.'*

So you just picked up lead guitar?
*'Yes, you have to, don't you? I had to make connections if I could. I
had a Spanish guitar and there was a Spanish guitar bit on* Gun Law,
*which reminded me of my guitar in some way, and I just felt it was
for me.'*

What were the first electric guitars that you had?
*'My brother had an electric one called a Club 40. My first electric
guitar was a bass guitar, called a Star – not a Framus Star bass. He
also had a Harmony guitar and I used that as a bass guitar. Then I
used it when I was first in the John Mayall group, as a lead guitar. It
was quite nice, worked quite well. Then I had a Les Paul.'*

Did you like the sound of the Les Paul?
*'No, I didn't really like anything but the cherry colour; it was a nice
colour and it was a sweet kind of design, And although it took me
back somewhere to Les Paul and Mary Ford – my brother had records
of theirs and I remember the guitar playing and the singing – I kind
of celebrated upon this guitar for some reason. Eric Clapton had one
and it looked nice and played good.'*

You say you saw the Rolling Stones and the Yardbirds. Where was that?
*'Oh, just floating around. They were scruffy and I enjoyed it because
I was scruffy as a kid and when you go to school you dress formally.
And anything to get out of that! the Rolling Stones were all scruffy, but
they had stylisation things.they used to wear things like waistcoats –
all stained and dirty, second-hand things – and it was just a giggle, it
was free. It was going away from school, anything away from the
school direction.'*

When did you first see Eric Clapton play?
'I first saw Clapton at the Crawdaddy club with the Yardbirds.'

Were you impressed?
'Yes, I loved it. I was impressed with his playing, but I was a bass player at the time, so I was listening to Paul Samwell-Smith more than anything. But the guitar playing was fabulous. Wow! He actually played it, not like the Rolling Stones and the Beatles, who were just filling in a solo, clunking along; the whole thing was a break. Do you remember that? The whole piece used to suddenly have a break, where the whole band goes into it, not just the guitar player.'

So you were playing bass?
'Yes, I tried to play like Paul Samwell-Smith. But when I first heard Bill Wyman in the Rolling Stones I started to try and play like him. I used to really enjoy myself, standing showing the other boys, "He goes like this", and holding the bass up like this; earnest, serious.'

Why did you swap to guitar?
'I actually started off playing the guitar, playing Shadows things, and then went on to bass. I was round this bloke's place one day and he had a Gibson bass guitar and I looked at it and thought, "Wow, electric bass guitar, what a fabulous-looking thing." It was all solid, four big strings, really kind of meaty, and I thought I would like to do that, so I went onto bass for a while.'

What got you back on to the guitar?
'It was the Yardbirds; the Eric Clapton movement.'

So he made you want to play the guitar again?
'No, nothing so personal; it was only to become professional. I was a bass player while I was at work, but I thought I might be able to find a professional group and play the guitar, because there weren't any good guitar players around. There was only Eric Clapton, who was

doing the blues thing and coming through on it. And it was nice, there's no doubt about it: it was gorgeous. So I thought I might be able to do that. I used to have a kind of saying that I would come alongside him in some way.'

What do you mean by that?
'Well, you know how good he was? The whole thing was that there was heart there; there was generosity there; there was a good person there. So I thought I maybe I could turn people on with a note of sadness. Like Satchmo – you know that kind of feeling. Well, Eric Clapton could do it, and John Mayall could do it, Aretha Franklin, the Staple Singers, all these people I started hearing. J.B.Lenoir is the master of that kind of thing. Eric Clapton did something like that and it might have coincided with something of mine. But the fact that I ended up taking over in a group that he left is not such a big inspiration as it was.'

How did that happen?
'I can't remember. I either followed up an advert in the paper or I put one in the paper and someone answered it.'

What was it like, being in the band after Eric?
'Fantastic.'

Did you play any of the songs that Eric had played?
'Yes, quite a lot of then.'

Like what? 'Hideaway'?
'No, I didn't do 'Hideaway', I did 'The Stumble'. It was similar, a Freddie King thing.'

Who did you listen to then?
'B.B. King, J.B. Lenoir, Robert Johnson, Elmore James. Millions of people! John Mayall used to play endless tapes, all different people; a hundred different people in one night. He had the whole of one wall

done with a tape recorder and he used to play all these different people.'

Did you enjoy playing in John Mayall's band?
'Sometimes.'

What times didn't you enjoy it?
'Well, I was so kind of behind. I was jumping the gun a bit. I was trying to play as good as Eric Clapton; I had to try because I had to fill his place. In the Yardbirds, when there was a solo break they all went in there and they all came out the other end. And it was nice, the proper thing. But then Eric started taking too many solos – maybe John Mayall pushed him into it, I don't know.'

Did he ever push you forward?
'Yes, he tried to. But I was just coming out of work, so I was pretty cold about going to the front if I couldn't handle it.'

Then you left John Mayall and formed your own band.
'I left John Mayall and I quit. I didn't know what I was going to do. I was floating around. I was going to go to Chicago and see If I could play some nice blues, where everybody plays together.'

How did you form Fleetwood Mac?
'Mike Vernon was the producer of Blue Horizon Records and he produced John Mayall. Mike Vernon introduced me to Jeremy Spencer.'

What were the first songs you wrote with Fleetwood Mac?
"Black Magic Woman', which I actually wrote when I was with John Mayall. I was living in John Mayall's house when I started to write that. John Mayall started me writing blues things; he said that I could do what he did sometimes. If you're singing or playing someone else's song and you really, really like it, if you're bubbling over with it, then you should take the first line and write another song. I did that thing,

148

a kind of symbol for a No. 1, or a hit record.'

Were you pleased when you had these hit records?
'Yes, it couldn't hurt me. It's a strange feeling. You kind of come over all exalted, if you allow it.'

How did you feel if you heard a record on the radio?
'Oh, I used to perk up.'

What about if you hear one today?
'Oh, I go through all kinds of performances. I usually take to the shadows and say a note of boredom upon it. Because I don't really think it's any good any more; I think it's old-fashioned.'

How did you come to write 'The Green Manalishi'?
'I nearly died one night, in my sleep. I don't know if you've ever had the experience; I've had it a couple of times and I'm inclined to think it's an experience that people have. But I was lying in bed, I was dreaming, and this little dog jumped up at me and it scared the shit out of me because this dog had died, and had been dead for a long time. It was a stray dog that I brought to the house and just looked after. And it was strange, kind of spooky, like voodoo. And it was a strange little dog. And I was dead and I couldn't move. I couldn't say 'I'm dead' – it wasn't available – so I just fought my way back into my body; I thought, "It must come alive", and it did. So I woke up and looked round – the room was really black – and I found myself writing the song. It was about money. The fear I got was that the reason this was happening to me was that I had earned too much money and I was separate from all people.'

So is that what the song says?
'Yes, the 'Green Manalishi' was money they still call it green-backs and things like that, don't they? When you haven't got any money you aren't worth anything to anybody.'

In the song it says, 'You come creeping around, making me do things I don't want to do'. Is that money?

'Yes, it goes off on a mythological definition level, but it starts, "You're the Green Manalishi with a two-pronged crown/All my trying is up, all you're bringing is down."'

How did you get the idea to do 'Oh Well'?

'Muddy Waters used to say, "Oh well, oh well."'

You used acoustic guitar on that, didn't you?

'Acoustic and electric guitar.'

Was it a Spanish guitar?

'No, a Michigan guitar, like a copy of a National.'

You eventually went to Chicago with Fleetwood Mac.

'Yes. Mike Vernon took us down South Side Chicago and I asked if we could play, see if we could sit in. It was great.'

You did some recording there?

'Yes, we did some recording, but it was only symbolic of being there. It wasn't much good. I think there was one good thing on it; I think it was one of Jeremy's songs. My stuff wasn't that good.'

Didn't you enjoy those sessions in Chess Studios?

'It was all right. It was another day, another freedom.'

You played with B.B. King, didn't you?

'That was sessions. I just turned up there one day – I didn't do much, just played on a couple of tracks. You can't do much with B.B. King because he's there doing the thing himself. He's not going to chop himself in half for me. This is this problem, again, with these impresario musicians; it's dangerous to follow them. I was very cautious about this; if I was going to have to be pinned to somebody, I

chose J.B. Lenoir because he had slave contacts and you could feel it. *He wasn't an entertainer from the entertainment world, that you could have on a cabaret show. He was pure, so I tried to hang in there.'*

Did you meet Jimi Hendrix?
'Yes, I bumped into him.'

Did you ever play with him, jam with him?
'Yes, twice. Once he took over from me in the Speakeasy; I was jamming with Eric Burdon and some other people. There was an interesting atmosphere around Jimi Hendrix. Very hard to discern briefly.'

Did you like his playing?
'Not particularly, no.'

Why? Was it too loud? Too fast?
'Too ahead of itself. If you didn't see that or you weren't prepared for it it could take you by surprise.'

Did you ever jam with Eric Clapton?
'Yes, a couple of times.'

How did that feel, since he was such a hero of yours?
'Nice. Oh, it was delicate, because you really are standing there, boy, and it's pins and needles. It really is strange. You know, is he going to wipe me out? If I play over the top, is he going to come back afterwards and leave me wiped out? A bit paranoid, those things are, a bit worrying.'

Do you still think of Fleetwood Mac as your band?
'No, I don't. I pulled out from thinking like that. They did sort of sniff in to the air to see if I was cool about what they wanted to do which was forget the fact that I was in the group now that I'd left. Well, I'm not in it any more and I didn't want to be in it, particularly.'

Do you still want to play now?
'Yes, as long as I'm not pushed or rushed, or forced into it.'

So what's the most important thing to you: that things are united and that no one is out front?
'The whole thing is that it's not important.'

It seems to bother you, talking about music.
'Yes, I think it's pointless.'

Why?
'It just is pointless talking about music because music is an opposing factor to talking.'

So you think people should just be able to listen to the music and not be interested in you as the maker of the music? But what if they are interested to see what you think, or feel? Do you think it's wrong for me to go up to someone like B.B. King and interview him?
'It kind of rushes us off our feet, you know? And it holds us up above you. But maybe I would like to sit and have someone like Otis Spann, Otis Rush, sort of telling me stories about things. Maybe I need that, maybe I've been without that. I wouldn't mind if I had someone sitting around, like Howlin' Wolf or Leadbelly.'

Why do you still play music?
'Because it's my living and it keeps me out of work – that's the only reason. I would always play music, though; I would have a guitar – I'm pretty sure about that. I might be much more into music if I hadn't become professional.'

Why did becoming professional stop you getting into music?
'Because you have to go a certain way; you have to follow a certain line to accomplish something. Although it was called the blues boom and all that kind of thing, to me it was still me learning the guitar

154

and trying something. But what kind of music would I have played if I hadn't gone professional? It would probably have been something different, like the Shadows, Hank Marvin, rock 'n' roll and the Beatles. But music is my career. So perhaps I am one of these characters that, on an island, would be a musician rather than a fisherman. Or, after the fishing was done, I would take to the music where others would sit around in corners, or dance.'

People say you don't try as hard any more when you play. Do you think you played better back then than you do now?
'Better than what? What do you mean by better?'

Well, if I listen to Fleetwood Mac records from the sixties, if I listen to John Mayall, I can hear you playing in a certain way.
'I don't think about it. I just play. So it comes back to what I was saying earlier on – which was how can you talk about music?'

But didn't you speak to B.B.King about his music?
'I asked him questions about religion. I wouldn't ask him about music or about his playing, because it's sacred ground.'

Why ?
'It just is, because they just look at you and wonder what you're talking about. What have they spent their whole lives playing music for? Is it for this, is it for that? Why do we have to speak? Why can't we play music? If I was working on a f***ing road drill you wouldn't walk up and say, "Why do you...?"'

I might if I wanted to know how it worked.

When you used to take LSD did you like it?
'You don't like it or dislike it. It's some kind of hellish neutrality, like sand, like gas, effervescent like Andrew's Liver Salts; you don't like it or dislike it but that turns you on in some way and LSD is like that.

But as you start to review your turn-on, it falls off and you're off the trip and back to normal – afternoon tea and biscuits, that kind of thing.'

You didn't take drugs when you were with Fleetwood Mac, did you?
'Yes. I used to smoke after gigs, but I was very cautious about smoking before I went on, because it was a bit of a fine line. I was a bit too sensitive. I found I was repeating myself. B.B. King repeats himself a lot, but he does it nicely so it's all right.'

When you're playing guitar now, do you enjoy it?
'No, because the music is so heavy nowadays that in big groups there's a conscious, "Is he going to make it?" kind of thing.'

Were you trying to reach the people when you were playing in Fleetwood Mac?
'No, nothing so flowery as that. Reach the people?'

How would you say it, then?
'Well, they were there; it was another night. They would be going to work the next day and I could see they were just ordinary people and you just pass another night with them. You've been there before, when you're in the audience and you have to go to school or work, and that's the way you passed that day. On that day you went to that concert.'

But to those people you became very special.
'Are you telling me that from a first-hand point of view?'

Yes, I am, because I've been in an audience and I've seen it. When I was eighteen years old I heard this guy called Peter Green and you became very special to me. So I'm not talking out of the top of my head, I'm talking about personal things of my life. And I think a lot of other people were the same, or else they wouldn't have bought your records,

would they?
'No. Unless it's just the record they liked. That's the way I always thought it was.'

This then is the entire text of my interview with Peter Green, which I include here because what I think he says is so relevant to the whole development of blues music into rock music at that time.

Eric Clapton and Cream

If Peter Green's Fleetwood Mac was the second band to form directly out of the Bluesbreakers then Cream was the first. Clapton, Bruce and Baker formed their group in 1966 and they performed along with Fleetwood Mac at the *Windsor Jazz & Blues Festival*. The name 'Cream' comes from the fact that they each believed they were the finest musicians on the scene at the time, so therefore they were the 'cream of the crop'.

Because of their individual reputations as musicians, they quickly gained a management and record contract with Robert Stigwood's Reaction Records and they were signed to Atlantic Records in the USA. As you will remember, Eric Clapton's original idea for the band was that they should become a blues trio. However, this was not to be.

Virtually straight from the word go the band started to gig. However, they soon discovered that they didn't have enough material and this apparently led to them starting to extend and improvise instrumental sections within pieces. These instrumental 'jams' became associated with the band. What in effect was happening was that Bruce, Baker and Clapton were soloing all at the same time. I can tell you from personal experience that to see these musicians jamming together in a small club or at a college concert gig was an awesome experience. Nobody had seen anything like it and although since those times critics have accused them of taking this to excessive levels it was very exciting at the time.

Cream's first UK release was a very strange choice; it was called 'Wrapping Paper' and as a track was as far away from a blues powerhouse trio as you could go. It had been written by Jack Bruce and a contemporary poet called Heat Brown. It did however, reach No. 34 in the charts. It was followed by another Brown/Bruce composition called 'I Feel Free'; now this was classic Cream stuff with a beautiful guitar solo from Eric Clapton.

The band's debut album – *Fresh Cream* – was released in the early part of 1967 and reached No. 6 in the UK album charts. I suppose you could describe it as a fusion of jazz and blues with a dash of pop music. However, the album contained plenty of instrumental high points. In March 1967, Cream were featured in a show in America hosted by Murray The Kay, called *Music Of The Fifth Dimension*.

It was during 1967 that the hippie psychedelic revolution began to makes its presence felt in America and Britain. This movement was associated with the anti-Vietnam protest movement, experimentation with various drugs and a general rebellion against materialism and society. It had started in San Francisco and eventually was to disintegrate as its members grew up and moved on. It did, during its time, produce many, many classic rock albums. Cream, as far as their American audience was concerned, were most definitely a part of this movement.

Beginning in April 1967, Cream toured the world endlessly, playing gig after gig – and they would eventually disintegrate as much from their exhaustion as from their musical differences.

At the start though, the first thing that Ginger Baker noticed was the immediate growth in the audiences at club dates compared to when he used to play with Bruce in the Graham Bond Organisation. Baker remembers:

'When we used to play with Graham Bond there would be four or five hundred people in the audience. As soon as we started gigging with Eric in Cream, there would be four or five hundred people locked out of the gig. I hadn't realised just what a big following Eric Clapton had.'

Fresh Cream reached No. 39 in the US charts and the band actually spent ninety-two weeks in the charts. On 2 July, 1967 Cream played at Saville Theatre on the same bill as the Jeff Beck Group and John Mayall's Bluesbreakers.

In December the group's second album, *Disraeli Gears*, hit No. 5 in the UK charts and broke through in the United States reaching No. 4. A single taking from *Disraeli Gears* called 'Sunshine Of Your Love', and featuring the famous bass riff and beautiful guitar solo from Eric Clapton, became their first US chart single, making No. 36.

In August 1968 the band released a double album, *Wheels Of Fire*, which combined studio recordings and live recordings. This album stayed at No. 1 in the US charts for four weeks. The release of the album in America boosted sales of the single 'Sunshine Of Your Love', which ended up selling over one million copies.

In September 1968, Cream split up as a result of sheer exhaustion. On 1 November, the band played Madison Square Gardens at the end of a farewell tour of America, and in London on 25th and 26th of that month the group played a farewell concert for their London fans at the Royal Albert Hall. They were supported by two new bands, one called Yes and the other called Taste. Taste featured a young Irish blues lead guitarist – a slide guitar virtuoso called Rory Gallagher. Rory played straight lead guitar much in the fashion of Buddy Guy and Albert King and was a second generation (Clapton and Green being first generation) British blues guitar hero, and one of the first players whose playing shows an obvious influence from Eric Clapton's performances with John Mayall and Cream.

The fact that the Royal Albert Hall farewell concerts were sold out shows just how popular Cream had become by that time. Eric Clapton and Ginger Baker went on to form a band called Blind Faith with Rick Grech on bass and Stevie Winwood on keyboard and vocals. At the time, this group was dubbed a super group. However, it didn't last long, and it was after this period that Eric Clapton's life was overtaken by heroin addiction.

Clapton's guitar playing in Cream reached new levels of power and experimentation. As if he needed it, it served to spread his reputation as a lead guitar player to an even larger audience, especially in the USA. Eventually, Eric Clapton was to have a major reaction – just as Peter Green had done – to the role of lead guitarist. Having heard an album by an American group called the Band, Eric gave up using Gibson guitars including the Les Paul and started to use the Fender Stratocaster with which he has been associated since that time.

During the seventies and eighties, long-time fans of Eric Clapton's blues guitar playing were driven almost to despair by his seeming lack of interest in being a lead guitar soloist. People began seriously to wonder whether he still had it in him anymore. But if you think about it, how could he have carried on under that much pressure. To go out on stage every night with an audience expecting that every solo you take is going to be some kind of classic statement would be an unbearable pressure for any musician – and so it proved for Eric Clapton.

Also, there was more to Eric than just his guitar playing. He had a genuine interest in song-writing and as a singer his voice has grown and grown in stature. I like his vocal performance on his recent *From The Cradle* blues album almost as much as his guitar playing which, although it still carries much authority, and because he is in middle age is far more mature, lacks (for me anyway) the attack and viscous quality of his earlier playing.

Anyway, I have always been a fan of his, as I am of Peter Green's and let's hope that Eric, who I am sure has a lot more great music in him, continues to record and play concerts.

Led Zeppelin

Back in the days of Cyril Davies and Alexis Korner's Blues Incorporated a young session guitarist was beginning to make his way. He was Jimmy Page. The London session scene was a very small closed shop, which meant that it was hard to get in to and was dominated by a more traditional kind of musician who could usually sight-read music and had a classical music training. However, with the advent of rock 'n' roll in the fifties and the subsequent skiffle craze, record producers were finding that they needed the services of guitarists who could reproduce the playing of American players like Scotty Moore, Elvis Presley's guitarist.

One of the first rock 'n' roll session guitarists was Big Jim Sullivan who played on numerous recordings, but he eventually found that he couldn't cope with the demand of his services and would therefore give work to Jimmy Page. Around that time, you will remember, Geoff Bradford had got to know Jimmy Page quite well and, indeed, Geoff had also done some session work sometimes even playing the harmonica.

After Eric Clapton left the Yardbirds, Jimmy Page joined the group subsequently switching to guitar. This meant that at one time the Yardbirds had two star lead guitarists: Jeff Beck and Jimmy Page. But Jeff Beck was soon to leave to form his own group, which left Jimmy Page as the lead guitar player.

In July 1968 the Yardbirds split up. Bassist Chris Dreja decided to form the new Yardbirds and the band was booked for a ten-day tour of Scandinavia. Jimmy Page was not happy with the line up of the band and decided to launch a new group. Dreja quit and became a photographer. Page recruited a fellow session musician called John Paul Jones to play bass. Having asked Terry Read and D.J. Wilson among others to join the group there had also been talk of John Entwhistle and Keith Moon joining Page from the Who – but all of this came to nothing since Read and Wilson also rejected Page.

Read however, suggested a nineteen year old Midlands rhythm and blues vocalist called Robert Plant for the group. Robert Plant suggested John Bonham as the drummer – and the band was complete.

In September 1968, this new band going under the billing of the New Yardbirds, fulfilled the previously booked Scandinavian tour. The group had taken on Peter Grant as their manager.

On 15 October, 1968 they made their debut as Led Zeppelin. The band got its name from a put-down by the Who's drummer, Keith Moon. Apparently at a party ,on hearing that Jimmy Page had recruited a couple of unknown musicians from out of town, he declared: 'Your band will go down like a lead zeppelin'. Jimmy Page, in a classic piece of inspiration, decided that he liked the name dropping the 'a' from the first word. He turned the insult into the name of the band.

The band recorded their first album in two weeks; it was released and simply entitled *Led Zeppelin*. In December 1968, the group began their first US tour and found immediate success. In many ways Cream had already paved the way with their recording success and both British and American audiences were more than willing to accept a new power group from England.

Now Robert Plant could really sing and brought to the music a love of American blues. He sang in the style of Howlin' Wolf, and Page, with his Les Paul guitar, proved to be a perfect foil for his on-stage performances. The rhythm section of John Paul Jones' bass and John Bonham on the drums brought together all the best qualities of the Fleetwood/McVie/Bruce/Baker rhythm sections of Fleetwood Mac and Cream.

In early 1969, the group's first album hit No. 10 in the US charts. It included two classic blues performances by the band of Chicago blues greats: Willie Dixon 'You Shook Me' and Otis Rush 'I Cant Quit You'.

In April 1969, Led Zeppelin hit No. 6 in the UK album charts. They adopted a unique policy of refusing to release singles in the UK preferring instead to rely on album sales. From 1969 until the death of their drummer John Bonham on 25 September, 1980 Led Zeppelin were by far the biggest heavy (rock) band in the world. Some idea of their power as a blues unit can be heard from their rendering of the blues 'When The Levee Breaks', which appeared on *Led Zeppelin IV*.

As a guitarist, Jimmy Page could be seen as one of the fathers of the modern rock lead guitar sound. As well as being interested and influenced by the great blues guitarists of Chicago, he was also a fine acoustic guitar player. As has previously been mentioned, running concurrently with the blues boon of the early sixties was a flourishing acoustic music scene. The previously mentioned Davy Graham was a pioneer of this scene, but the arrival of Bert Jansch gave it one of its major stars.

Jimmy Page later described Jansch as 'a real dream weaver' and Jansch's playing was influential in the development of Jimmy Page's own acoustic guitar style. What Jimmy Page did with Led Zeppelin was to combine elements of acoustic guitar with blues lead electric guitar playing fusing them together in to his own lyrical and mercurial phrases. Dave Gilmour of the progressive rock band Pink Floyd was to use a similar fusion though with a different result in his work with that band.

What we are increasingly seeing is the blues lead guitar style refined and popularised by Eric Clapton, which we first hear in the classic John Mayall's *Bluesbreakers featuring Eric Clapton* album, being taken by other guitarists and used in a variety of different fusions as lead guitar against varying types of music.

Free

In 1968, in the middle of the Cream/Fleetwood Mac emergence, another band began to form that had direct connections to two of the main characters in our story, John Mayall and Alexis Korner. This band's name was Free and featured a guitarist who was at the time eighteen years old – Paul Kossoff.

Kossoff combined in his guitar playing many of the qualities of Eric Clapton and Peter Green. He used the Les Paul guitar as had Eric Clapton and Peter Green and his sound was very close to that of Eric's on the *Bluesbreakers* album. However, his phrasing and his timing were far more like Peter Green's. Tragically, Paul Kossoff was to become a victim of drugs and he died of heart failure on a flight to New York on 19 March, 1976. He was twenty-six years old. This then is the story of Free...

The band consisted of Paul Rodgers on vocals, Paul Kossoff on guitar, Andy Fraser on bass and Simon Kirk on the drums. They were all roughly of the same generation. Andy Fraser had joined the band having been fired from John Mayall's Bluesbreakers. Alexis Korner who, as ever, was an encouragement to the group having seen their first gig, gave them the name of Free. In the sixties, Alexis had a trio at one time to which he gave the name Free At Last, so perhaps he got the idea from that.

In November 1968, the group signed to Ireland Records, which was by that time a leading independent record company with a reputation for quality. Chris Blackwell, who had formed this company, grew up in Jamaica and had released many reggae records from that country in the UK during the sixties. The band's first album was called *Tons Of Sobs*, which did not chart in the UK.

In 1969, they released a single called 'Broad Daylight'. By this time they were beginning to get a large reputation through their almost non-stop touring of the UK club circuit. Their popularity was extended to the United States when in September 1969 they toured there supporting the Eric Clapton/Jack Bruce super group Blind Faith. It wasn't until July 1970 that the band were to really break through. This was a result of the release of a single called 'Alright Now', which has within it one of the most famous guitar riffs in rock music. The sound of this single is reminiscent of Cream at their more laid back and 'Alright Now' was a hit in the UK charting at No. 2.

Having released their second album, *Free,* in November 1969 (which reached No. 22 in the UK charts), the band followed it up in August 1970 by releasing *Fire And Water,* which included the hit single 'Alright Now'. The band then played the *Isle of Wight* rock festival – a kind of British Woodstock at which Jimi Hendrix among others also appeared. Because of the impact the band made at the festival and because *Fire And Water* included their hit single, this album reached No. 2 in the UK charts.

In October 1970, 'Alright Now' was a hit in the United States reaching No. 4 in the charts; the album *Fire And Water* reached No. 17.

The follow-up single released in January 1971 was called 'Stealer'. It climbed to No. 49 in the US charts, but was not a hit in the UK. In February the same year the new album, *Highway*, reached No. 41 in the UK, but only managed No. 190 in the US charts.

On 9 May, 1971 due to friction between the members of the group and an obvious disappointment at the lack of sales of *Highway*, the group split. Subsequent to this their record company released *Free Live*, which was a hit in the United Kingdom reaching No. 4 in the charts and was more successful in the United States than their previous release, charting at No. 89.

Paul Kossoff and Simon Kirk, meanwhile, had completed their own project releasing an album *Kossoff, Kirk, Tetsu And Rabbit*, keyboardist John 'Rabbit' Bundrick and bassist Tetsu Yamauchi joining Kossoff and Kirk in this short-lived venture.

In January 1972, Free reformed and toured the UK. They also began to record together. *Free At Last*, the new recording, was a hit at No. 9 in the UK and reached No. 69 in the US. A single, 'A Little Bit Of Love', taken from the album was a UK hit at No. 13.

In June 1972 the group toured the USA. During this tour guitarist Paul Kossoff began to suffer from the effects of drugs and became erratic as a performer, completely missing out on several gigs. This was all too much for Andy Fraser who left to form a new group called Sharks immediately before Free's tour of Japan.

By this time Paul Kossoff's drug problem had caught up with him and he was unable to take part in the Japanese tour. It was then that Tetsu and Rabbit were recruited and Paul Rodgers played guitar. In October, Paul Kossoff was fit again and rejoined the band for the UK tour and to record an album. But he soon left Free for good to pursue his own solo project and released an album called *Backstreet Crawler* – a name he would subsequently use for a band that he formed in 1974 after signing a record contract with the American-based Atlantic Records.

In February another Free album, *Heartbreaker,* was released by Ireland Records and was a hit in the UK achieving a No. 9 position. It also rose to a respectable No. 47 in the American charts. In July 1973, Free officially split up again. In August of that year, Ireland Records re-released 'Alright Now' and it re-charted in the UK reaching No. 15.

Due to the continuing popularity of the band Ireland Records quite naturally continued to release products; therefore in 1974 the compilation *Free Story* was issued, reaching No. 2 in the UK album charts. A year later a similar compilation called *The Best Of Free* was released in the United States only, but reached no higher than No. 120 in the charts. One year after that, Kossoff died from that heart attack.

Over the years the band have maintained a popularity with successive generations of rock bands. The death of Paul Kossoff robbed the guitar community of someone who would, I'm sure, have continued to make a major contribution to the electric guitar art form had he lived. You should check out a Free CD, and if you listen to Kossoff's guitar playing you will hear a wonderful combination of the playing of those two ex-Bluesbreakers Green and Clapton, against the vocal performances of Paul Rodgers who as a singer came to rival in the public's mind Robert Plant of Led Zeppelin. Rodgers' vocal performances stand comparison with Peter Green's singing at its best, both in Rodgers ability to transmit emotion and his timing.

Recording studios in the sixties

At the beginning of the sixties, recordings of groups were made in an entirely different way to the practice that was to become accepted at the end of that decade. This fact played a major part in the development of the rock art form and, as we shall see, the Bluesbreakers album featuring Eric Clapton in no small way changed the rules for producers and sound engineers when it came to making records.

In the early days of the sixties a blues band like Blues Incorporated or Long John Baldry's Hoochie Coochie Men would go to the studio with the specific intention of simply putting on to tape their live concert repertoire. In the studio the engineer and producer would use a multitrack machine, which usually had the capacity to record either four tracks completely separately, or in some cases three tracks. This meant that recording was like having four (or three) separate tape recorders running at the same time.

For example, you could could record a band's rhythm section on one track, then play that back to the singer who would add vocals. So far we have used two tracks. Then the horn section, sax players and so on could put down their contribution on a separate track... So now we have used three tracks. Finally, the lead guitarist could put down his contribution on the last remaining track. Wouldn't it have been nice if it was that simple?

In many instances the band would not like working in this way, preferring to take the more natural route of playing all their instruments together as an ensemble, just as they would do at a concert. This was to present the recording engineer with a problem, especially if the producer decided that he wanted to reserve the right to re-record the vocal on a separate occasion with the band not present. A reason for the producer doing this would be that he might not have been happy with the original vocal performance and rather than using up studio time by getting the whole band in again he would simply re-do the vocal.

Technically, to achieve this the engineer would try to make sure that the original vocal performance was on a separate track and could not be heard on the band's rhythm track so that it would be easy to replace. In the event of the producer wanting to use the original vocal performance put down with the group live in the studio, the studio engineer would have to be even more careful during the initial recording.

The problem would be one of what is called 'spill'. Spill refers to sound spillage which takes place if the instruments are played too loud. What happens here is that some of the sound of the band, which ideally should only be heard on the one or two tracks of the four-track tape used by the engineer to record them, could spill over on to the vocal track which might be, let's say, track three. Therefore, recording engineers were forever pleading with musicians who wanted to use amplification in the studio (absolutely essential for the new blues bands) to keep the volume down. This could even apply to drummers with the engineer suggesting that the drummer change his pattern of playing so as not to hit those loud symbols too hard.

This, of course, had a radical effect on the sound of the band, which eventually found its way on to record. Hence the early blues fans' constant lament: 'I got the record, but the band sound much better live'. Considering the facts it's hardly surprising, eh?

Unfortunately the studio scene, which was dominated by the engineer and producer, was in reality a bit of a dictatorship. Geoff Bradford remembers these times very well:

'What happened was you went in the studio, you played your stuff and you did exactly what you were told and then you were out again. They were always watching the clock because time in the studio cost money. All you could do if you were in a band was hope that you played OK and that the engineer and producer would do a good job. You were totally powerless as far as influencing the sound of what eventually got released.'

And now you can see exactly what the fundamental contribution that album John Mayall's Bluesbreakers Featuring Eric Clapton made to the sound of recorded blues guitar. In one moment of time it turned everything upside down. I mean, the point was that the album sounded really great and from that moment onwards all the guitar players wanted to be able to play their guitars with the proper sound coming out of the amplifier in the studio, so that their audience would be able to hear them in a similar way to when they were playing live.

Of course, Clapton's use of the Les Paul and the new Marshall amp was also an innovation, but as you will remember Eric insisted on playing flat out. This did lead to a confrontation between engineer Gus Dudgeon and Eric Clapton, but because Eric was already such a star, and because John Mayall definitely didn't want to upset Eric, and also because John Mayall realised how important Eric's sound was to the way he played, Mayall made sure that Clapton prevailed.

John's comment at the time to the engineer and producer (Mike Vernin), was 'give God what he wants' – an attitude for which all us subsequent guitarists should be eternally grateful to Mayall.

After these times multitrack tape recorders began to arrive on the studio scene: first eight-track and then sixteen-track recorders began to revolutionise the scene.

It's ironic to note that in modern times many musicians feel that this whole process has gone too far in the other direction. Bands are now trying to record in a more live situation in the studio attempting to capture the excitement and energy of live performances. Because of the growth of digital studio technology during the eighties, many recordings, although technically almost perfect on hearing, lacked something of the spontaneity of the earlier classics.

Going back to the recordings made by the classic American blues bands in Chicago in the late forties and all through the fifties, these recordings would have been made almost entirely in one take and completely live.

One could spend an endless amount of time enjoyably speculating as to what might have happened to the sound and quality of the Chicago bands and to the sound of the Cyril Davies and Alexis Korner combinations, had the studio revolution happened ten years before it did.

Lastly, just a note about the early recordings of the country blues guitarists and singers such as Blind Lemon Jefferson, Leadbelly and Robert Johnson. These were made on old-fashioned recorders that looked like the phonographs that played 78 rpm records in the twenties and thirties. What you did, especially in the early days, was to actually sing down the sound horn – and the disc was cut there and then.

Very shortly after this, an electrical system was introduced that allowed the use of a microphone, but this was still a very primitive sound compared to today. The effect on the ear is to make the music and vocal performance sound compressed giving these early recordings a somewhat tinny characteristic. Once you have heard this sound, even when it's reproduced on CD, you never forget it and it acts as a kind of a mystical sound screen through which we hear the music of those times.

169

During the sixties there was a breed of record collector who was convinced that these recordings with *that* sound were the only really genuine blues records. Crazy, isn't it!

Chapter 18

Pop music in the UK...
The blues reaction

In America the growth of rhythm and blues in the fifties – both in its black manifestation through the likes of Muddy Waters and so on, and in its off-shoot rock 'n' roll performed by the likes of Little Richard and in the white version by people like Bill Haley & The Comets – was to have an influence in the UK on the development of pop music. In the UK of the fifties, pop music performers tended to be squeaky clean. People like Adam Faith, Marty Wilde and Cliff Richard represented an appeal which was firmly aimed at teenage girls.

The arrival of the Beatles in the early sixties marked a watershed in the development of British pop music. A new generation of fans represented a new market. The Beatles began by wearing smart suits and they had neat haircuts, but as we have seen earlier in the book, they were soon challenged for the affections of the hearts of young ladies by a somewhat rougher band by the name of the Rolling Stones. However, throughout the sixties there was always a breed of young men who reacted against all of this 'trivia', finding solace in the blues.

The British blues movement really has no precedent anywhere else in the world. In London, there was a whole set of fans that had little or no idea as to the lifestyles of the black musicians who had invented this art form, and to be quite frank this lack of knowledge didn't matter to them at all. It did matter to John Mayall though, hence his album entitled *Crusade* in which he tried to draw the attention of the press and the public to the contribution that he felt these black artists had made.

Undoubtedly though, for these young white blues fans it was the likes of Clapton and Green that caught their imagination. As we have seen, the London blues scene was strange and almost like a secret society at the beginning. If for American blacks the blues had been an outpouring of emotion directed at and resulting from their harsh treatment within American society, as well as being an entertainment, then the London blues scene was sustained by a much milder reaction, but no less profound in its outcome by young English males against the day-to-day triviality of their lives.

In America the black audience soon left the blues behind, moving on to the soul music of Aretha Franklin and Otis Redding, the more pop sound of Tamla Motown and on into rap.

In both the USA and the UK it is the enthusiasm of successive generations of white blues enthusiasts that has kept, and continues to keep, this legacy available on CD to the public in general. For many American blacks, and probably for British ones as well, the blues is synonymous with being a second-class citizen. Whether this will ever change remains to be seen.

John Mayall was, and is, a great populariser of the blues and he surely must be gratified to have seen his enthusiasm for this once obscure art form taken up by so many.

Discography

If you want to follow the musical route that led to the Bluesbreakers, here are some suggestions for albums you might want to try to get hold of. I have kept the selection entirely to CD (compact disc) format, as records and tapes are becoming increasingly more difficult to find in many cases.

So that you can use this discography as a stand-alone section I have also included a brief summary of each artist's significance on the trail that we have followed. For more details you can refer back to the relevant parts of the book.

CHARLEY PATTON

Undoubtedly the first significant Mississippi Delta blues man to record. A great influence on many of the most important players to blaze the blues trail including Robert Johnson, Muddy Waters, Son House, Bukka White and Howlin' Wolf. Charley Patton is also renowned for being one of the first blues men to have been reliably documented as having lived 'the blues life'. Legend has it that he had his throat cut in a bar room fight and that even though he was a small thin man, he was always ready to start a fight given an excuse. During his life he appears to have had an on/off relationship with religion. His powerful voice seemed to belie his small stature. However, to listen to his 'Pony Blues' is really to experience the fountain head of the Delta blues style.

CDs to listen to:

Founder Of The Delta Blues (Yazoo 1020)

King Of The Delta Blues (Yazoo 2001)

SON HOUSE

A contemporary of Charley Patton and part of his circle, Son House was perhaps the major influence on Robert Johnson. His blues were, if anything, even more intense than those of Charley Patton. Rediscovered in the sixties, Son House became the inspiration for many of the white folk blues guitar players of that time who came to prominence.

CDs to listen to:

Father Of The Delta Blues (Columbia Legacy 471662)

Death Letter (Edsel ED CD 167)

The Complete Library Of Congress Sessions 1941–1942 (Travelin' Man TM CD 02)

Delta Blues (Biograph BCD 118)

SKIP JAMES

Worth a listen for two reasons: his vocal style, which finds some resonance in the singing of John Mayall; and his unique and haunting guitar work. The guitar work displays the kind of emotion that we later hear in the performances of Peter Green. After his re-discovery in 1964, and his well-received performance at the Newport Folk Festival, he remained a popular performer on the blues/folk circuit. Cream were to record his 'I'm So Glad'.

CD to listen to:

Greatest Of The Delta Blues Singers (Biograph BCD 122)

BUKKA WHITE

Another musician who was greatly influenced by Charley Patton. Bukka White was an animated performer and you really must try to hear some of his recordings. They are full of conviction and aggression and if Robert Johnson represented the sound of the haunted blues player standing at the crossroads, then Bukka White's playing is reminiscent of the aggression he might have experienced on a bad night at the juke joint. After shooting a man in a 1937 bar-room incident, it was Alan Lomax who helped him to get him out. Led Zeppelin were to record his 'Shake 'Em On Down'.

CDs to listen to:
Sky Songs (Arhoolie CD-323)
Baton Rouge Mosby Street (Blues Beacon BLU-10032)
Also check out:
Roots Of Rock (Yazoo 1063)

ROBERT JOHNSON

Just about *the* most influential Delta Blues musician on the white blues scene both in America and the UK – and most likely throughout the rest of the world as well. Robert Johnson was simply a brilliant guitarist, songwriter and blues performer. Not much more needs to be said, except he is essential to any blues collection.

Really the only CD set to get is:
The Complete Recordings (CBS 467246 2)
Absolutely fantastic...

MUDDY WATERS

It was Muddy Waters who became the premier South Side Chicago blues band leader. Another musician whose influence cannot be over-emphasised, especially with regard to the early London blues scene. In Muddy we see the transition from rural acoustic blues to urban electric personified. There's tons and tons of Muddy Waters material available on CD, but there's one I think you should check out, especially because of its influence on Cyril Davies regarding his decision to form his own blues band.

That CD is:
Muddy Waters At Newport (MCA/Chess CHD-31269)
You should also try to purchase:
The Chess Box (MCA/Chess CHD3-80002 (US))

This recording profiles Muddy Waters in his Chicago days. The set also features guest appearances from musicians such as Rory Gallagher, Paul Butterfield and Mike Bloomfield.

CHICAGO BLUES SCENE IN GENERAL

There are numerous compilations available, but perhaps the best are the Chess box sets and compilations, and you should check these out.

LITTLE WALTER

You should check out Little Walter as much for his influence on white blues guitar sound as for his undoubted harmonica prowess. You see, it's my contention that his performances had an influence, even if somewhat subliminally, on the bluesbreaker sound in general. He was one of the first harmonica players to use the harmonica with a microphone – with devastating results. His highly explosive harmonica playing in the Muddy Waters Blues Band, and in his own right, are reminiscent for me of Eric Clapton's equally explosive playing on the John Mayall's *Bluesbreakers* album.

You should try to get hold of:

Blues With A Feeling (Charly CD BM 23)

This recording has got a good cross-section of Little *Walter's genius well displayed.*

J.B. LENOIR

J.B. Lenoir arrived in Chicago shortly after Muddy Waters, and his high vocal tone is reminiscent of the singing of Skip James. J.B. Lenoir became a favourite of John Mayall, who recorded his own tribute to J.B. called 'The Death Of J.B. Lenoir'. J.B. Lenoir is also noted for the fact that he composed many blues that departed from the normal 'boy meets girl' and 'I have been betrayed' themes. Notable is the 1952 single 'Eisenhower Blues', which was a vicious attack on the newly elected president.

Try to get hold of:

Alabama Blues! (L & R/Bellaphon CDLR 42001)

BLIND LEMON JEFFERSON

One of the first really successful blues artists in terms of record sales, Blind Lemon Jefferson has also been mightily influential. The likes of Howlin' Wolf, T-Bone Walker, Lightenin' Hopkins, B.B. King and Muddy Waters all came under his influence one way or another. Before his death in 1929, he had enjoyed fantastic popularity.

CDs to listen to:
King Of The Country Blues (Yazoo 1069)
Blind Lemon Jefferson (Ace CDCH 399)

BLIND WILLIE McTELL

Blind Willie McTell's 'Statesboro Blues' became one of the most performed blues songs by white blues rock combos during the late sixties. Famous for his twelve-string guitar playing, Blind Willie McTell was also a fine bottle neck guitarist.

Try to find:
The Early Years 1927–1933 (Yazoo 1005)
1927–1935 (Yazoo 1037)

BLIND BLAKE

Along with Rev Gary Davis, Blind Blake is remembered first and foremost as an acoustic guitar finger-picking virtuoso. Blake recorded what was essentially the dance music of his time, and he also recorded what could be seen as novelty songs, such as 'Diddie Wa Diddie' and 'Skeedle Loo Doo'. However, you really must listen to this man's fantastic guitar-picking virtuosity. Blind Blake and Gary Davis were two of the first performers whose guitar playing reputations really caught the public's imagination.

The CD to get is:
Ragtime Guitar's Foremost Fingerpicker (Yazoo 1068)

At this point I would like to include two performers who you should also check out because they were so influential in the early London blues scene – both for those musicians who were to follow the electric path and for those who were to stick primarily to the acoustic guitar.

MISSISSIPPI JOHN HURT

Now Mississippi John Hurt is really an oddity. A farmer for the whole of his life, he seems in 1928 at the age of thirty-six, to have recorded two sessions – one in New York and one in Memphis – and then disappeared again. However he was re-discovered in the early sixties and it was through the recordings he did at that time that he achieved instant fame and became so influential. His influence remains very strong, even to this day. He was a beautifully laid-back performer, and quite different from virtually every other blues performer of his generation. He was more of a songster than he was an out-and-out blues performer.

You can hear John Hurt's 1928 recordings on:
1928 Sessions (Yazoo 1065)
However, you should definitely check out:
The Best Of Mississippi John Hurt (Vanguard VMCD 7304)
This contains those wonderful sixties recordings that he made after his re-discovery.

BIG BILL BROONZY

When Eric Clapton was just starting out on guitar, one of the acoustic guitarists he first got into was Big Bill Broonzy. Virtually all of the notable acoustic guitarists who were around in the early days of the London blues scene all listened to, and learned from, Big Bill Broonzy – notably, Geoff Bradford. You can hear an acoustic recording called 'Hey Hey' recorded by Eric Clapton on his unplugged album, which was originally written by Big Bill Broonzy. Another musician who should be seen as a serious guitar virtuoso, this aspect of Broonzy's talent is often overlooked. For me he fits into the same guitar circle that might include Blind Blake, Blind Boy Fuller, the Rev Gary Davis, Broonzy himself and Brownie McGhee. There are lots of Broonzy recordings available...

For his guitar playing check out:
Do That Guitar Rag 1928–1935 (Yazoo 1035)
For a general look at his later work try:
Remembering Big Bill Broonzy: The Greatest Minstrel Of The Authentic Blues (BGO BGCD 91)

BLIND BOY FULLER

Another great finger-picker, Blind Boy Fuller was a very successful blues recording artist of the late thirties – and you should try to get hold of some of his music. When Brownie McGhee started out, he was at one point whisked into the studio shortly after Fuller's death and billed as Blind Boy Fuller No. 2 – a crude attempt to capitalise on Fuller's reputation. However, as has already been pointed out McGhee, along with the Rev Gary Davis, will always be associated with Blind Boy Fuller.

Here's some listening suggestions:
East Coast Piedmont Style (Columbia Legacy 467923 2)
Truckin' My Blues Away (Yazoo 1060)

REVEREND GARY DAVIS

One of the finest guitar finger-pickers of all time, the Rev Gary Davis was also a purveyor of 'Holy Blues', as he used to describe it. He was a street preacher in New York City when he was discovered. Although he had a very rough vocal style, which probably derived from all those years of trying to compete with traffic noise, his guitar playing is a revelation.

You should check out:
Pure Religion And Bad Company
(Smithsonian/Folkways SF 40035)
You should also try to get hold of:
Blues & Ragtime (Shanachie 97024)
This CD contains some fantastic performances recorded between 1962 and 1966. By the way, the Rev Gary Davis was also one of the earliest

noted guitar masters to give guitar lessons. Two
of his more well known students were Stefan
Grossman and Ry Cooder.

LEADBELLY

Leadbelly, whose fantastic twelve-string guitar work should be
heard by anyone interested in the guitar or the blues in general, is a
true legend of the blues. His tough-guy reputation is reminiscent of
Charley Patton. However, the big difference is that Leadbelly was a very
big man and the kind you wouldn't really want to upset. Like Patton, he
lived the blues life and was in and out of prison on a number of
occasions before ending up as a chauffeur for Alan Lomax. Leadbelly
was never a particularly successful seller of records, but he was a
mighty performer of the art. He was also a fine slide guitarist as you can
hear if you check out his performance of 'See See Rider Blues'.

Here are some CDs to check out:
The Very Best Of Leadbelly (Music Club MCCD 106)
Midnight Special (Rounder CD 1044)
For the more folky sound of Leadbelly try:
Leadbelly Sings Folk Songs (Smithsonian/Folkways CD SF 40010)
It is worth noting that Leadbelly's performance of
'Mama Did You Bring Any Silver' (*aka* Gallis Pole)
was re-interpreted and recorded as 'Gallows Pole'
by Led Zeppelin.

BOOGIE-WOOGIE PIANISTS

The boogie-woogie piano players were a great influence on Geoff
Bradford, Alexis Korner and John Mayall.
Try to check out some of their playing on:
From Spirituals To Swing (Vanguard VCD2-47/48)
This features great performances from Albert Ammons
and Meade 'Lux' Lewis.
You can hear the playing of Cow Cow Davenport on:
Barrelhouse Blues 1927–1936 (Yazoo 1028)

Two more albums worth a listen are:
Piano Blues Vol. 1: The Twenties (1920–1929) (Story of The Blues CD 3511-2)
Piano Blues Vol. 2: The Thirties (1930–1939) (Story Of The Blues CD 3512-2)

So now on to electric guitar players...

B.B. KING

B.B. King is undoubtedly *the* most famous of the black American lead guitar players and he has a tremendous number of albums available on CD.

I would recommend you try:
King Of The Blues (MCA CAD4-10677)
This is a four CD set, which will give you a really good overview.

You should also try to get:
Live At The Regal (MCA MCAD 31106 (US))
This is an import album, but it is one of the most influential electric blues albums to ever have been released.

Check out, if you can:
Blues Is King...Plus (See For Miles SEECD 216)
This was recorded in a small club and contains some fine examples of B.B. King's slow blues guitar style, whose influence you can see on the playing of Peter Green.

FREDDIE KING

Both Peter Green and Eric Clapton listened to and recorded instrumentals and songs by Freddie King. What Freddie King's guitar playing had was attack, and a certain kind of funky sound.

You should check out:
Texas Sensation (Charly CD Charly 247)
This contains many of the classic Freddie King recordings.

While we are on the subject of Freddie King, try playing back-to-back Freddie King recordings with Eric Clapton's performance on the *Bluesbreakers* album. Much is often made of the influence of the black American players on Eric Clapton's guitar style, but here's an opportunity to note just how unique Clapton's own playing had become. Sometimes comparisons are helpful, and while you are doing this try the same technique with Peter Green. Most instructive.

ELMORE JAMES

In my opinion Elmore James has been underestimated as a serious performer. You should check out his contribution and make up your own mind, but for me his performance of 'The Sky Is Crying' is as haunting as any performance you will hear in the blues. Everyone, of course, has recorded his material including Fleetwood Mac, The Yardbirds and Jimi Hendrix, and you can see his influence in the playing of Lowell George of Little Feat and in the sound of Ry Cooder and Johnny Winter. Elmore James is another musician from the Charley Patton school of emotion and aggression... wonderful!

Here are some CDs to check out:
The Immortal Elmore James: King Of The Bottleneck Blues
(Music Club MCCD 083)
Let's Cut It: The Very Best Of Elmore James (Ace CDCH 192)

BUDDY GUY

Buddy Guy is yet another tremendously influential musician. However, he can be somewhat of an erratic performer, reminding me very much of guitarist Jeff Beck. I have seen them both perform many times and, along with Jimi Hendrix, if we are being honest we have to say that on a bad night, they were very bad, but on a good night they could transcend the blues format and take you into new and exciting areas. Despite his long career and much praise from everyone – including notably Eric Clapton and John Mayall, who have both performed with him – Buddy Guy seems somehow never to have quite found his own audience. However, you can help in this matter by rushing out and buying a Buddy Guy CD!

Two current albums you should check out are:
Damn Right I Got The Blues (Silvertone ORE CD 516)
Feels Like Rain (Silvertone ORE CD 516)
The latter includes a performance by John Mayall
on 'I Could Cry'.

Another good recording is:
Stone Crazy Chess (CD RED 6)
This features Guy's earlier recordings made
during the sixties.

T-BONE WALKER

Widely credited as the origin of the contemporary electric blues lead guitar sound. T-Bone Walker is a must for your collection. His playing has in the opinion of many critics, never been equalled and certainly he is a complete master of timing and of the double-time guitar lick. For me, though, his playing remains in a sort of box of its own. No one else quite sounds like him, although it's obvious that his playing has been re-interpreted by many others. One reason for getting hold of a copy of a CD of his playing, as far as this book is concerned, is the fact that he was such a *big* favourite of Geoff Bradford. A comparison of the playing of Geoff Bradford on 'Long John's Blues' (BGO Records; full catalogue listing given later in Geoff Bradford's section) and that of Eric Clapton's on the *Bluesbreakers* album bears comparison with the difference between Freddie King's playing and that of T-Bone Walker. The point about T-Bone Walker is that there hadn't been anything like him before; he really is the start of the whole line that leads, as far as our book is concerned, to the playing of Peter Green and Eric Clapton.

Here are some T-Bone Walker CDs:
Low Down Blues (Charly CD CHARLY 7)
Includes perhaps his most famous composition,
'They Call It Stormy Monday (But Tuesday's Just As Bad).
T-Bone Shuffle (Charly CD BM)

HERBERT SUMLIN
Check out CDs by Howlin' Wolf because, for years, Sumlin was Wolf's
guitar player.

HOWLIN' WOLF
A larger than life figure and a fantastic vocalist, Howlin' Wolf was the
only serious contender to Muddy Waters as far as status was concerned
on the Chicago blues scene of the forties and fifties. As a blues force,
Howlin' Wolf was almost elemental and definitely fits into the line that
runs from Charley Patton through Son House and Robert Johnson.
Here we have another major influence on the early London blues
scene, and it is in Wolf's recordings that we can hear the playing of
Herbert Sumlin who was such an influence on Geoff Bradford.
Everyone knows Wolf's 'Smokestack Lightenin', 'Backdoor Man',
'Spoonful' and 'How Many More Years', and it seems that most bar
blues bands have tried this stuff at one time or another. Howlin' Wolf
seems to combine, for me anyway, the raw sound of the country blues
of the Delta region with the driving sophistication of the Chicago
South Side electric blues. Wolf is essential for your collection.
Here are some CDs:
Howlin' For My Baby (Sun CD CHARLY 66)
The Chess Box Set (MCA/Chess CHD3-9322 (US))
Finally check out:
The London Howlin' Wolf Sessions (MCA/Chess CHLD 19167)
This recording features contributions by many of Wolf's
fans on the English scene such as Eric Clapton,
Steve Winwood, Charley Watts and Bill Wyman.

JOHN MAYALL
In this book we are concentrating on the two John Mayall's
Bluesbreakers albums, which are obviously essential for your collection
and for any understanding of the twisting plot of our book.
They are:

John Mayall's Bluesbreakers featuring Eric Clapton
(Decca Deram CD 800 086-2)
A Hard Road (Decca London CD 820 474-2)
You should also check out two other John Mayall CDs
which feature music of the time:
John Mayall's Crusade (Decca Deram 820 537-2)
Blues From Laurel Canyon (Decca Deram 820 539-2)

The first of these recordings introduces the playing of the young guitarist Mick Taylor who had the unenviable task of replacing both Clapton and Green in the Bluesbreakers. To be perfectly honest, Mick Taylor's performance on this set cannot really be compared to the performances of Peter Green and Eric Clapton because his guitar playing was at an early stage of development. The second of the two recordings is the better to hear Mick Taylor on as far as a John Mayall context is concerned. By this time John Mayall had dropped the Bluesbreaker tag from his support band, but Mick Taylor's playing on this album shows a development and maturity. For more Mick Taylor performances check out his time with the Rolling Stones.

FLEETWOOD MAC, CREAM, JIMI HENDRIX
You have probably got many of the albums by these bands in your collection already. Jimi Hendrix's first album contains his classic recording of his own blues 'Red House', which bears comparison with the best of Chicago Blues. As far as Fleetwood Mac is concerned, you should check out particularly the...
'Live in Boston' set called:
Boston Live (Castle Classics CLACD 152)
It contains many fine live recordings.

This discography has been a brief look, but obviously there is a wealth of material out there for you to continue to explore and with which to enrich your blues life.

JOHN MAYALL BLUES BREAKER

Sources

The Big Book Of Blues, Robert Santelli, Pavilion Books, 1994.
Blues In Britain, Bob Brunning, Blandford Books, 1995.
Blues On CD, Charles Shaar Murray, Kyle Cathie Ltd.
Book Of Rock Stars, Dafydd Rees & Luke Crampton, Guinness, 1991.
Clapton, Edge Of Darkness, Christopher Sandford, Victor Gollancz, 1994.
The Complete Rock Family Trees, Pete Frame, Omnibus Press, 1993.